You and Your Money

You and Your Money

A Guide from God's Word

Ron Hembree

BAKER BOOK HOUSE
Grand Rapids, Michigan 49506

Reprinted 1981 by
Baker Book House with
permission of copyright owner

ISBN: 0-8010-4252-6

Printed in the United States of America

Scripture passages quoted are from The King James Version of The Holy Bible, and from The Living Bible: Holman Illustrated Edition. Those taken from The Living Bible are so indicated in the text of this book.

To
Mark Buntain
a special friend
who weeps for our wounded world

Contents

Preface

Profits of Doom

Just as marriage does not create problems, but reveals them, so hard times bring to light the deficiencies in ourselves and our society. Thus, with the reality of double-digit inflation and an ever-increasing worry about money, there is now an intense proliferation of prophets of doom and prosperity preachers.

On one hand there are economists who predict total collapse of our economic systems. On the other hand some are saying these are the "seven fat years" and now more than any other time in history is when we can make great profits and live like a "king's kid." Just as a river runs between two banks, so the truth is probably somewhere between these two extremes.

There is no doubt that many countries of our world are in deep financial trouble. While North Americans struggle with a double-digit inflation rate, some nations with less stable governments have even greater problems. Israel, for example, last year had a staggering inflation rate of 50.6 percent with no relief in sight. Not only do we have to deal with spiraling inflation but its twin sisters, unemployment and physical want.

That many in our world are deeply concerned is most evident. For one thing Howard J. Ruff's dismal book, *How to Prosper During the Coming Bad Years** was for a good time on top of the bestseller's list. *Time* magazine called him a "*profit* of doom" telling how he has cashed in on the very real economic fears of our worried world. Ruff's book has been reprinted several times and there seems to be no end of sales in sight. He also started a newsletter (Ruff Times) that soon had 80,000 subscribers paying $125 each for fifteen months of his morbid advice. His second annual convention on financial survival drew over five thousand worried fans, and this self-taught economist now commands over $3,000 per lecture. His half-hour syndicated television talk show (Ruff House) is carried by forty-eight stations throughout the United States.

Ruff has come by his views legitimately. A college dropout, he has been affected by a checkered career as a singer, actor, stock broker, owner of a speed-reading franchise, natural vitamin distributor, and real estate investment teacher. A decade ago he was $250,000 in debt after his speed-reading school failed and he had to declare personal bankruptcy. However, today Ruff has made a fortune and says he has paid off all but three of his creditors. He admits, "Some people said that I couldn't succeed at anything, so I became a prophet of doom." Then he adds, "This nation is ripe to be manipulated by a powerful personality. I am appalled at the ease with which I am acquiring a following."

Standing on the other bank from Ruff and his ilk is the prosperity preacher who promises the Christian he can confess anything his heart desires and be assured of receiving it; almost like having a verbal credit card without any payment responsibilities. This is an oversimplification, but it is true that some religionists seem to be irresponsible in their blanket promises of prosperity. Their promises even have a ring of political rhetoric like "a chicken in every pot." However, the rhetoric has been upgraded to "a Cadillac in every garage."

---

* Howard J. Ruff, *How to Prosper During the Coming Bad Years.* (Don Mills, Ontario: Fitzhenry & Whiteside, 1979).

Because of these conflicting views, some people are asking, "What is the truth?" The only answer we have to that is, *Thy Word is truth* (John 17:17). Thus, the purpose of this book.

There are great principles of prosperity in God's Word, and there is His tremendous promise that the believer will not only survive bad times, but also thrive during crises: *They shall not be ashamed in the evil time: and in the days of famine they shall be satisfied* (Psalm 37:19). However, for this great promise to be fulfilled there are conditions; just as there are fixed laws that must be known and obeyed if prosperity is to result. We never really break the laws of God, we only break ourselves on them.

Thus, if the believer prospers during the bad times that one day will surely come, he must be practicing the principles of God's Word. That is why, twice, God says, *My people are destroyed for lack of knowledge* (Hosea 4:6). Again, *Therefore my people are gone into captivity, because they have no knowledge: and their honourable men are famished, and their multitude dried up with thirst* (Isaiah 5:13).

Ethel Waters said it best: "God don't sponsor no flops." However, for us to actualize that concept we must be aware of, and obedient to, the great principles of prosperity in God's Word. Prosperity will not just happen. The principle of our universe is sowing and reaping, cause and effect. This is why Joshua warns, *This book of the law shall not depart out of thy mouth; but thou shalt meditate therein day and night, that thou mayest observe to do according to all that is written therein: for then thou shalt make thy way prosperous, and then thou shalt have good success* (Joshua 1:8).

Therefore, the purpose of this book is to explore those great principles of prosperity found in God's Word. If we do, then, *When thou passest through the waters, I will be with thee; and through the rivers, they shall not overflow thee: when thou walkest through the fire, thou shalt not be burned; neither shall the flame kindle upon thee* (Isaiah 43:2).

Ron Hembree

1

Why God Wants You to Prosper

"Why do you wear such new clothes while millions of people are starving?" screamed cult leader Jim Jones to the cowering woman standing embarrassed before him and the People's Temple Planning Council.

In the spate of books that have flooded the market since the "Guyana Massacre" authors and ex-members of the cult are exposing how Jones kept control by such emotional outbursts and intimidation. But even though we recoil in horror at the events, and the mind control of Jones' death cult, the question he asked seems to be a legitimate one posed by many concerned and caring people in our society. How can the Christian church justify its excesses in the full face of the ugly want and hunger of our sick world?

Stanley Mooneyham recently asked, "What do you say to a hungry world?"

This question becomes even more uncomfortable when we realize that while half of the world is dieting, the other half is starving. How can we speak of prosperity in the face of gnawing hunger? It is a question that will not go away.

Our family recently visited Calcutta, India. I shall never forget our ride from the airport into the entrails of that "city of the dreadful night." We had been warned there would be hunger and sorrow, yet nothing we had read or heard had prepared us for some of the horrible things we saw. Babies with starvation-bloated stomachs pulled hungrily on the milkless breasts of emaciated mothers. Hollow-eyed men shuffled through the bowels of the disease-infested city seeking some type of employment so they could buy a bowl of rice for their hungry children. The filth, the sickness, the heartbreak, forced me to conclude that if Calcutta were not hell, at least it was hell's front porch.

I looked around at my traveling companions to see their reactions to this panorama of human horror. A doctor and his wife were with us. He became red-faced with anger seeing the filth and human deprivation. His wife talked in illogical circles, trying to verbally erase the hell before her eyes. My son sat in stunned silence barely able to comprehend the pathetic parade. I looked at my wife and she sat silent with great tears washing down her face.

Is it not true that in the face of such awful poverty it would be almost blasphemous for us to talk of prosperity? How can we speak of desiring comfort when sixty percent of those in India live on one meal per day. The vast majority of children there must subsist on less than 900 calories per day; about the equivalent of two Milky Way bars.

Yet, strangely enough, it is that scene of horror that has driven me to write this book about prosperity. The want of our world is not God's desire. His great heart is broken more than ours could ever be over the hurts and hungers of our aching world. And therein is the reason God wants us to prosper.

We Are God's Post Offices

God's Word clearly tells us why He desires to pour great blessings and prosperity upon us. He has chosen us as channels through which He can heal the hurts of our wounded and dying world. This great concept is best articulated in Psalm 67 where the Bible says we are to be God's post offices; that is, we deliver God's letters of love and concern to a waiting world through our care and concern for others. The psalmist says, *God be merciful unto us, and bless us; and cause his face to shine upon us.* Then without ending the sentence he explains why he presumes to pray this seemingly selfish prayer, *that thy way may be known upon earth, thy saving health among all nations* (Psalm 67:1, 2). Clearly the purpose of prosperity is not to pamper God's people, but that the saving health of God may be proclaimed and actualized on the earth. God wants us to prosper that we might have resources to bind up the wounds of our dying world.

From the beginning of Israel God called the Jews to be a "chosen" people. Some have misunderstood that calling thinking it meant they were God's pets. However, even a limited understanding of the Bible cuts through that false assumption. Israel was chosen for two reasons: First, to live the laws of God and prove by their lives that this is the highest, happiest, and healthiest way to live, and second, to share these laws with the rest of the world our Lord loves. If Israel ever refused to fulfill this responsibility the Bible warned, *He will surely violently turn and toss thee like a ball into a large country: there shalt thou die, and there the chariots of glory shall be the shame of thy Lord's house* (Isaiah 22:18).

Could it be that the horrors Israelites suffered through the centuries were because they forgot their calling? Clearly God expects responsibility from us who have received so much. His Word declares, *For if God spared not the natural branches, take heed lest He also spare not thee. Behold therefore the goodness and severity of God: on them which fell, severity; but toward thee, goodness, if thou continue in his goodness: otherwise thou also shalt be cut off* (Romans 11:21, We are called as Christians for the same two purposes.

The Bible talks much and often of our hurting world. Paul says, *For we know that the whole creation groaneth and travaileth in pain together until now.* Paul looks forward to the great day of redemption when the pain is past, saying, *And not only they, but ourselves also, which have the firstfruits of the Spirit, even we ourselves groan within ourselves, waiting for the adoption, to wit, the redemption of our body* (Romans 8:22, 23).

But while we are waiting for ultimate redemption we can do something about the hurts of humanity. The Bible says, *Because the creature itself also shall be delivered from the bondage of corruption into the glorious liberty of the children of God*

(Romans 8:21). Thus, we can do much to reduce the pain by introducing mankind to the Great Physician.

Jesus captures the same sense of responsibility when He says, *For unto whomsoever much is given, of him shall be much required: and to whom men have committed much, of him they will ask the more* (Luke 12:48). Prosperity does not come to the believer to give him more creature comforts, but rather that he, in turn, can bring comfort to other creatures.

Building on this basic premise the psalmist says, *Let them shout for joy, and be glad, that favour my righteous cause: yea, let them say continually, Let the Lord be magnified, which hath pleasure in the prosperity of his servant* (Psalm 35:27). When God's servants respond by being responsible, God desires to bless them more. He knows the more He gives to them the more resources they have to reach the lost world He loves. The rationale for increased prosperity is that there be an increase in reaching the lost with the glorious gospel of Christ. A Christian's commitment therefore must keep pace with his increased prosperity, and it is urgent to keep this proper perspective.

If we ever make appreciable gains in solving the sorrows of our world, it will be because we not only feed the body, but also the soul. Both blades of the scissors are necessary to have a cutting edge. So, it is imperative that we not only take man out of the slums, but also the slums out of man. This is what prompted famed preacher Henry Drummond to write, "It is idle to talk of Christ as a social reformer if by that is meant that His first concern was to improve the organization of society, or to provide the world with better laws. These were among His objects, but His first was to provide the world with better men."[1]

Drummond then goes on to cogently consider, "The Kingdom of God is a society of the best men, working for the best ends, according to the best methods. Its membership is a multitude whom no man can number; its methods are as various as human nature; its field is the world. It is a Commonwealth, yet it honors a King; It is a Social Brotherhood, but it acknowledges the Fatherhood of God. Though not a Philosophy the world turns to it for

---

1. Henry Drummond, *The Kingdom*. (London: Collins, 1930) pp. 88, 89

light; though not Political it is the incubator of all great laws. It is more human than the state, for it deals with the deeper needs; more catholic than the church, for it includes whom the church rejects. . . . This mysterious society owns no wealth, but distributes fortunes."[2]

Isaiah noted long ago that when the Kingdom of God comes into a man's life, the end result is that his world becomes better. *And the work of righteousness shall be peace; and the effect of righteousness quietness and assurance for ever* (Isaiah 32:17). Then the great silver-tongued preacher rushes on to add, *And wisdom and knowledge shall be the stability of thy times* (Isaiah 33:6).

Christ's program deals with the real world. It is not an escape from reality, but confronts reality with the life-changing and thus a world-changing truth. Our world is writhing in agony, regardless of how comfortable we personally may feel at any given moment. The old poet was right:

There is no flock, however watched and tended,
But one dead lamb is there;
There is no home, howe'er defended,
But has one vacant chair.[3]

Think of our wounded and waiting world — not just of its surface — but of the very real world as it is; as it sins and weeps, curses and suffers, and sends up its long cry to God. Limit it if you wish to the world around your door, but think of it. Think of the city and the hospital and the jail and the grave; of the cold and the cruelty. Think of the fever, the famine, the ugliness, the loneliness, and the pain. And then try to keep down the lump in your throat as you take up His Word and read:

The Spirit of the Lord is upon me,
because he hath anointed me to preach the gospel to the poor;

---

2. Ibid., p. 81
3. Ibid., p. 76

he hath sent me to heal the broken-hearted,
to preach deliverance to the captives,
and recovering of sight to the blind,
to set at liberty them that are bruised,
to preach the acceptable year of the Lord
(Luke 4:18, 19).

God wants us to prosper so that we may reach His lonely lost children dying in the cold night of sin without warmth. Understanding this fundamental principle we appreciate prosperity as a tool to build a better world. And, lest we forget, the gospel is really the only antidote to the infection of our dying world. The more we learn the more we understand that *want is a spiritual problem.*

2

Want Is a Spiritual Problem

The church has often been castigated because it has talked about "pie in the sky" and ignored the need for a bowl of real rice now. But the charge is a foolish one. We must never misunderstand that the basic problem of our world is a spiritual one. Thus, it has a spiritual solution.

The gospel is ever practical. The real believer not only talks of the "sweet bye and bye," but also moves to minister in the nasty "here and now." Faith and works have always been inseparable. They are like the two oars of a boat; of equal importance.

James says, *What's the use of saying that you have faith and are Christians if you aren't proving it by helping others? Will that kind of faith save anyone? If you have a friend who is in need of food and clothing, and you say to him, "Well, goodbye and God bless you; stay warm and eat hearty," and then don't give him clothes or food, what good does that do? So you see, it isn't enough just to have faith. You must also do good to prove that you have it. Faith that doesn't show itself by good works is no faith at all — it is dead and useless. But someone may well argue, "You say the way to God is by faith alone, plus nothing." Well, I say that good works are important too. For without good works you can't prove whether you have faith or not; but anyone can see that I have faith by the way I act* (James 2:14-18, Living Bible).

Thus the real believer sees the bleeding of our world and moves to help; but merely putting bandages on wounds is not enough —

there must be something done to stop the raging sickness that creates the open sores. We can't continue to merely drain off the poison. That is why works must be accompanied by faith, for humanitarianism alone is not enough. We can not only give a loaf of bread in His name, we must also introduce the sick ones to the One who has life everlasting and can change their present world.

Lest we misunderstand about hunger and want being a spiritual problem, let us reconsider. An enigmatic verse in the Bible says, *but money answereth all things* (Ecclesiastes 10:19). There have been many attempts to explain this very difficult reference. Some scholars claim it was a tongue-in-cheek comment by the cynical preacher. Perhaps it was, but it is still truth. To explain its meaning, let us look again to the swollen and infected land of India to see clearly that its overwhelming economic problems have a spiritual origin. This is but one example. In seeing this, we understand that *money answereth all things.* The economic well-being of a nation is determined by the foundation on which that society is built.

Admittedly there are severe problems in India. It is true that 90 percent of that country's wealth is in the hands of 10 percent of her people. We also know that 60 percent of Indians can neither read nor write. The Indian national newspaper freely admits that over 60 percent of the work force is child labor. Vast farmlands are arid because of lack of irrigation. Ninety percent of India's water dumps into the ocean because "earthcutting" is a low-caste job. Rather than dig irrigation ditches, people starve. Rats eat much of the crops produced by the small farms, and these rodents are not killed because of religious superstition. Oxen still pull plows, and mechanization is virtually unknown. Add to all this the fact that *over 685 million people* live on a land space one-third the size of the United States.

But looking beyond these staggering statistics the careful observer will see that at the root lies a spiritual problem; for Hinduism teaches its adherents to escape reality, not confront it. One of its cardinal doctrines is, "Lord Krishna steals and captivates the hearts of his devotees, making them *forget* the world; draws their minds toward his blessed feet, and makes them enjoy everlasting peace and bliss."

The foundation stones of Hinduism are reincarnation and karma. These ideas are wrapped tightly together, one unable to stand without the other. The Hindu believes in being "reborn." In fact, when you talk with one about being "born again" he agrees. But he does not mean the same thing as the Christian. To him, being reborn means to visit this earth again and again in different bodies. His rebirths permit him to better himself, until he reaches a state of bliss.

One of Hinduism's leading gurus says, "Christians believe that one life determines and settles everything. No opportunity is afforded the sinner to purify himself in later births. How can this be? How can the everlasting future of man be made to depend on one small, insignificant life? Should he not get his chances for correction and improvement? The doctrine of reincarnation is quite rational. It gives ample chances for man's rectification, growth, and gradual development."

Obviously the Hindu religion teaches that man must purge himself. There is no forgiveness. If he has sinned, he must pay. And that payment comes in the form of reincarnations. If a man has been bad in this life, then next time around he will be born a rat, or a snake, or a bird, or an insect. He might even be born a demon. If he has been good, he might be born into a higher caste. Some time in the far distant future, he might even arrive at Atman, "where you will be freed from the round of births and deaths. Freed from sin, freed from passion, you become a liberated sage." However, the Hindu guru warns, most people are mixtures of good and bad, and therefore they never rise above their caste; never escape the endless cycle of births and deaths.

There is a despair about Hinduism. "Man corrects and educates himself," the gurus say, "through sufferings, pains, sorrows, troubles, difficulties and disease; through loss of property, poverty, and death of near and dear relations." Thus, to deprive a person of suffering is to deprive him of his education.

Married to this despairing doctrine is "karma," or fate. Swami Sivananda explains karma by a simple illustration. He says there are three parts to karma: accumulated works, fructifying works, and current works. He says these can best be explained by the simple picture of an archer. On the archer's back he has a quiver of arrows; in his hands, a bow with an arrow ready to shoot. He has already shot one arrow, and it is now traveling through the air.

The Swami explains that the quiver of arrows is "accumulated works." These represent all a man's talents, abilities, intelligence, and personality. How many arrows he has depends on the activities of past lives he has lived — the better his lives, the more arrows.

The arrow poised, ready to shoot, represents "current works." He can still decide where to aim. This means the deeds he does today will come back, either to haunt or bless him, in future lives.

But the most diabolical part of karma is represented by the arrow already dispatched. This is "fructifying karma." This arrow represents a person's present position in life. The caste in which he was born, the money he does or does not have, the illnesses he suffers — all these have been determined by previous lives, and there is no way to stop an arrow in flight. The only way an arrow can be stopped is for it to be expended. It must continue on its journey until it drops to the ground. This means the Hindu is hopelessly locked into his lot of life. He can never hope to escape from the harshness of his lonely existence. And he believes that every other person is experiencing his own "fructifying karma." To help another person would be to interrupt his karma and take it upon himself.

Understanding this foundational doctrine, the true Hindu sees a baby starving and says, "He must have caused someone else to starve in a previous life. The best thing I can do is let that baby experience his fructifying karma, so he can return in another form." If a woman is being raped, it means she has raped someone else in a former life. This also applies to murder and robbery and every other vicious crime.

It must have been this damnable philosophy that prompted the psalmist to exclaim, *Have respect unto the covenant: for the dark places of the earth are full of the habitations of cruelty* (Psalm 74:20).

It was a wise man who said, "To study comparative religions, don't get a book, get a ticket. Travel to those places of the earth that have not yet been touched by the gospel, and see the death and despair there."

India reels under the staggering effects of its religion and superstitions. Such philosophy keeps the country in bondage and fear. To merely feed the hungry would not solve the overwhelming problem; there must be a change of heart. The old ideas of superstition must be torn down so a new order of love, concern, and care can be developed. Only then can these people be free.

India is a classic example of what the Bible meant when it said, *Much food is in the tillage of the poor: but there is that is destroyed for want of judgment* (Proverbs 13:23).

Understanding that man must change from the inside out, rather than the outside in, God tells Jeremiah, *See, I have this day set thee over the nations and over the kingdoms, to root out, and to pull down, and to destroy, and to throw down, to build, and to plant* (Jeremiah 1:10).

Cure cannot come to a person or a country until the old ideas and philosophies die. Only after the ground has been plowed up and stripped of debris can a crop be planted. This is why India's problem will never be solved until her people have been freed from superstitutions that blind their brilliant minds and keep them in bondage.

Some of the earth's most brilliant people are Indians, so it is not ignorance that keeps them hungry. Rather, it is a spiritual blindness. Paul said, *But if our gospel be hid, it is hid to them that are lost: In whom the god of this world hath blinded the minds of them which believe not, lest the light of the glorious gospel of Christ, who is the image of God, should shine unto them* (II Corinthians 4:3, 4).

If poverty and pain result from a spiritual problem, then there is a spiritual solution — a solution that includes both bandaging the wounds and stopping the infections. This is why the Bible says, *Righteousness exalteth a nation: but sin is a reproach to any people* (Proverbs 14:34).

Thus the principles of prosperity we have learned so far are: First, God wants to bless us so we can help heal our wounded world. Second, poverty results from sin and separation from God.

Having learned these two facts we move on to discover that prosperity comes directly from God.

3

Your Paycheck Comes from God

"Spider" Rolland said it best. Over a decade ago the late political pundit commented on bureaucracy by noting, "Government is like a log floating down a swift river on which there are 2000 termites, each termite believing he alone is steering it."

It is true that most world governments have become so massive and cumbersome that they are guided by events rather than "steered" by capable leaders. Thus most governments are "reactionary," insofar as their leaders are constantly reacting to some crisis, and sticking their fingers in leaking dikes. Not much time is left to them for thoughtful and sure leadership. So, there seems to be little hope that galloping government spending will ever get under control or that we will ever catch up with runaway inflation. Many world leaders worry that we are rushing into an economic Armageddon.

In such a time it seems that everything that is nailed down is coming loose. Many in our world are in panic with a "machine gun" mentality. They are hoarding food, gold, silver and guns, awaiting a world holocaust they are sure is coming very soon. In this climate of "careless" concern it is urgent that believers turn to God.

God Is Our Source

This concept seems simple enough until we try to "put the sermon into shoe leather." Then it becomes more difficult because many so-called "leading economic advisers" are telling us just the opposite. They say our economic welfare is tied to Arab oil — or a political party. If we listen to them, perhaps we should hoard, and take care of "number one." However, God's Word warns, *Be not afraid of the words that thou hast heard, wherewith the servants of the king of Assyria have blasphemed me* (Isaiah 37:6). Regardless of what the economic indicators say, or the prophets of doom predict, God is still our source.

Much of the tension of the Christian life was taken out of my life one day when I read Hebrews 12:2. Like most Christians I worried and fretted about my spiritual and physical welfare, then God's Spirit taught me, *Looking unto Jesus the author and finisher of our faith.* It was easy for me to admit Christ gave me my faith, but the greater lesson was that it is also His responsibility to finish my faith. In other words I am God's problem.

Now admittedly, this concept should have been crystal clear long before then. After all, David had noted, *The Lord is my shepherd; I shall not want* (Psalm 23:1). Sheep have need of three things: pasturage, water and rest. To find all three in the desert country of Israel was not easy. However, it was not the sheep's responsibility, but the shepherd's. The sheep's only chore was to follow.

So, with our spiritual lives, our Lord is the giver and sustainer of our faith. If we get out of line it is His chore to correct us. This is why Hebrews 12 was written, to let us know how He, as Shepherd of our souls, provides, protects, and perfects us. Clearly He is our Source. And, what is true in the spiritual is also true in the physical. God's Word is replete with the concept that all the material blessings we possess are gifts from our God.

Riches and Honor Come from God

David had lived a long and eventful life. There had been shadows as well as sunshine. He had downed his Goliath, only to be felled by a bathing woman. He had risen to heights of sacrifice in extraordinary acts of greatness and compassion. But, he had also shown his meanness and pettiness to Abigail. Now, he is at the other end of life's road. About to die, he takes his battle-scarred crown off to place it upon the head of his brilliant son Solomon. Interestingly enough the last words we hear from the lips of David are a prayer. And in that prayer for Solomon, David shares a magnificent truth: *Both riches and honour come of thee, and thou reignest over all; and in thine hand is power and might; and in thine hand it is to make great, and to give strength unto all* (I Chronicles 29:12).

David knew that while man scrambles and competes for wealth and worth, these come only from God. He alone is our source.

Health and Wealth Come from God

Some, unthinking, might respond: "I work hard for my money. What do you mean, God is our source?"

The question is too unnecessary to even merit an answer, but we need to remind ourselves that God says our ability to make and retain wealth is in His hands. *But thou shalt remember the Lord thy God: for it is He that giveth thee power to get wealth.* Then Moses moves on to remind Israel again of the purpose of prosperity: *that he may establish his covenant which he sware unto thy fathers, as it is this day* (Deuteronomy 8:18).

Without the health, power, and mentality God gives us we could neither amass wealth nor retain it. Moses writes again, *And ye shall serve the Lord your God, and he shall bless thy bread, and thy water; and I will take the sickness away from the midst of thee* (Exodus 23:25).

The promise is simply that as our lives are obedient to Him, He will bless us with health to get wealth. As we will see in a later chapter the believer has a much better chance for sustained health than the unbeliever. While God does not promise immunity from all the vicissitudes of life, the follower of Christ does have tremendous advantages. The general principle is, *If thou wilt diligently hearken to the voice of the Lord thy God, and wilt do that which is right in his sight, and wilt give ear to his commandments, and keep all his statutes, I will put none of these diseases upon thee, which I have brought upon the Egyptians, for I am the Lord that healeth thee* (Exodus 15:26).

Not only is God the source of wealth, health, and honor, He is the Master of Life's everchanging circumstances. This is why He promises that even the elements will work in favor of the faithful follower of Christ: He promises *rain in due season.*

The Source of Circumstances

Although it seems farfetched, God's Word promises that the elements will work for the follower of Christ. Moses quotes God to His people: *And it shall come to pass, if ye shall hearken diligently unto my commandments which I command you this day to love the Lord your God, and to serve Him with all your heart and with all your soul, That I will give you the rain of your land in his due season, the first rain and the latter rain, that thou mayest gather in thy corn, and thy wine, and thine oil. And I will send grass in thy fields for thy cattle, that thou mayest eat and be full* (Deuteronomy 11:13-15).

Lest this sound too Pollyannish, the believer must realize that Christ is the Master of the elements — the story of the calming of the sea should forever settle that question. But, there is more. We all realize that cataclysmic events happen to the believer and the unbeliever alike. The question comes, "How do we reconcile this?"

Jesus frankly admits, *for he maketh his sun to rise on the evil and the good, and sendeth rain on the just and on the unjust* (Matthew 5:45). Doesn't this cancel out the promise of God to Moses? No, for the Bible also notes, *but time and chance happeneth to them all* (Ecclesiastes 9:11). We all understand that life is so structured that storms do come — but, the one who builds on the rock is not victimized by the storm. He stands strong through it.

God's Word promises that His followers are never victims, only victors. This is why Paul says, *We are troubled on every side, yet not distressed; we are perplexed, but not in despair; Persecuted but not forsaken; cast down, but not destroyed* (II Corinthians 4:8, Part of man's misunderstanding comes because he often reads texts and not the Bible. He studies theology, instead of studying God's Word.

We know that troubles do come, but the overriding promise is rain in his due season. That is, even the angry elements will work for the believer. It is why Paul says, *And we know that all things work together for good to them that love God, to them who are the called according to his purpose* (Romans 8:28). As believers we are never "under the circumstances," rather we are victorious over them. And in all time, good or bad, God is the source of the believer's circumstances.

The Storm Reminds Us

But still, the larger question is, "Why the storm?"

Again the Bible has the answer. The old preacher writes, *In the day of prosperity be joyful, but in the day of adversity consider: God also hath set the one over against the other, to the end that man should find nothing after him* (Ecclesiastes 7:14). At times we can become too worldly-minded. Sometimes in lying down we find this is the only time we look up. Therefore, *He maketh me to lie down* (Psalm 23:2).

There is a strange alchemy in human tears that washes away our pretensions and pride, causing us to focus once again on the really important issues of life. So Shakespeare was right when he wrote:

> *Sweet are the uses of adversity;*
> *Which, like the toad, ugly and venomous,*
> *Wears yet a precious jewel in his head;*
> *And this our life, exempt from the public haunt*
> *Finds tongues in trees, books in running brooks,*
> *Sermons in stone, and good in everything.*

Promotion Comes from the Lord

Without question, the hardest lesson for us to learn in understanding our source is that our promotions come from God. Of course our society and free enterprise system attempt to refute this. They tell us that promotion results from hard work, political intrigues, knowing the right person, and being in the right place at the right time. But the Bible insists, *For promotion cometh neither from the east, nor from the west, nor from the south. But God is the judge: he putteth down one and setteth up another* (Psalm 75:6, 7).

If Christians grasp that concept it will take much of the tension out of their occupations. They no longer try to please the boss, but do their work as unto the Lord. Thus, they become better workers; more responsible, more conscious, and ever greater in skill. Also, the bitterness of being overlooked in times of promotion doesn't debilitate them. They understand the source of their promotions is not their earthly boss, but their heavenly Father who sees in secret and rewards openly. They know when He desires them to move up, and when He thinks they are ready He will set before them an open door which no man can close. They also understand that if He closes up one source of income He will open another, since He is the ultimate source.

God is the source of our wealth, health, circumstances, and our promotion. But this is a lesson we must learn over again each day, since it is in total contrast to the world system. That is why Paul reminds us, *And be not conformed to this world: but be ye transformed by the renewing of your mind, that ye may prove what is that good, and acceptable, and perfect will of God* (Romans 12:2).

Perhaps a vivid word picture would permanently etch these great truths into our minds. The picture comes from an ancient wise man, dead nearly twenty-five centuries. His name was Zechariah and he saw visions. One of these is most poignant. We know it as the vision of the man with the measuring line.

Zechariah lived during a tense time in Israel's history. The people had returned from Babylonian captivity and were struggling to reestablish their homeland. To help them do this God sent two prophets, Haggai and Zechariah. Haggai was old and sharp tongued, while Zechariah was younger and a quiet intellectual. In one of Zechariah's many visions, a young man moves through Jerusalem with a measuring line in his hand. An angel sharply rebukes the youth saying, *Jerusalem shall be inhabited as towns with-*

out walls for the multitude of men and cattle therein: For I, saith the Lord, will be unto her a wall of fire round about, and will be the glory in the midst of her (Zechariah 2:4, 5). With that, the vision suddenly breaks off like an old movie with a broken reel.

Three Things Were Wrong

Although we might struggle to understand the dream, Zechariah knew exactly what it meant. The youth was rebuked by the angel because three things were wrong. The first was that the boy wanted to build the walls, before the temple. The place of worship was to be at the center of their political and religious life, and God, clearly called for Israel's allegiance to Him first. But, the boy was being disobedient. Afraid because of innuendos and threats from hostile neighbors, Israel decided to disobey God and build a wall before building a temple. Their priorities were wrong.

Society changes from the inside out, not from the outside in. Modern man may feel that he has enough money to clear the slums, to better man's education, to create a better climate of concern, and by doing so he will have a "great society." But this is building the wall before the temple. Educating the sinner merely makes him a smarter sinner. Nothing is done about the evil inside and it is from the evil within that crimes emanate.

Charles Colson, converted after his shabby Watergate dealings, confessed, "I have spent a lifetime in government and have never once seen government change a single person. Only Christ can change a man." Educator Mark Kennedy freely admits that education can at best only modify behavior, not change it. But, man seems to constantly need to reinvent the wheel. When will we learn that we simply cannot change society by changing conditions? There must be an inner change first.

The second thing the young man in Zechariah's vision did was to misunderstand God's purpose for Israel. The boy wanted to build a wall. However, walls not only provide a measure of protection, but they also imprison. And we must remember that man's way is always exclusion; God's way is expansion. God never intended His people to wall themselves up on an island. Rather, He wanted them to move among the masses bringing a healing touch and hope to humanity. That is why God's Word says, *Enlarge the place of thy tent, and let them stretch forth the curtains of thine habitations: spare not, lengthen thy cords, and strengthen thy stakes; For thou shalt break forth on the right hand and on the left* (Isaiah 54:2, 3).

The lesson of Jonah is that God desires that all men come to know him. Jonah was too clannish and tried to relegate God to a tribal deity. God is the Father of all mankind. His burning question to Jonah in that poignant last chapter is simply, "How can you care for the gourd, when thousands are dying outside my love?"

We must never forget that God blesses us to expand His kingdom, not to retreat to some safe harbor just to wait out our years on this earth in comfort and protection.

Finally, the third thing the youth did wrong was even to think of building a wall. God says He wants to be our protection, *I . . . will be . . . a wall of fire round about, and will be the glory in the midst of her.* We try to protect ourselves against the vicissitudes of life, yet in reality, God is the ultimate source of our safety. There is not a wall in the world high enough to keep us from getting hurt. The Bible says, *Except the Lord build the house, they labour in vain that build it: except the Lord keep the city, the watchman waketh but in vain* (Psalm 127:1).

This lesson finally penetrated my own consciousness when I was half a world away from home. One lonely night, I was especially worried about my family's safety, and not being able to sleep I picked up God's Word and read: *The horse is prepared against the day of battle: but safety is of the Lord* (Proverbs 21:31). Like the knight of old I had taken all precautions for my family's welfare. Now I needed to rest in Him and realize that ultimately, protection comes from God. He is our source.

Thus, in Zechariah's vivid word picture we see three things.

- We must build the temple before the wall, or that man changes from the inside out.

- God's way is expansion, while man's way is exclusion. We must be a missionary people.
- God is our source of wealth, health, circumstances, promotions, and safety.

No wonder David said after he had been in the fold of the Great Shepherd that he never wanted to live anywhere else. Once we taste of God we are spoiled for everything else.

If God is our source, then our obedience to Him will open the windows of Heaven for his blessings, and our disobedience will close those windows. Our personal prosperity depends on our relationship with God, so our disobedience creates financial crisis — not only for us, but for those all about us.

4

How Sin Costs You More than $5 Per Day

Jahandar Shah emerged as eighth Moghul emperor of India and reigned only eleven months before being strangled at the feet of his beloved dancer and mistress. He was a degenerate monarch who did much to bring down the powerful rule of the Moghuls who had dominated old Hindustan for many centuries.

Turning the elegant Moghul court into a brothel, Jahandar Shah gave over his powers to a prime minister who made havoc of the government, while the emperor and his mistress passed their hours in idleness, tossing rocks at passersby from the roof of the Red Fort in Agra. Another favorite pastime was having boats sunk in the Jumna river so they could enjoy watching women and children drown en masse. Needless to say, when the evil emperor was assassinated there was little weeping in the land.

It is easy to see how the misdeeds of rulers can bring havoc to a nation. Fortunes can be erased at the stroke of a pen. Lives can be forfeited with the nod of a head. Careers carefully molded over the years can be ruined by the rap of a gavel. Irresponsibility of leadership can and does bring heartbreak to thousands of subjects. Yet, we do not always realize that our own sin brings grave consequences not only in our lives, but to those about us.

No man is an island. He is touched by and touches many others. That is why we cannot sin without hurting someone. We cannot steal without depriving an innocent party. We cannot murder without destroying life, and we cannot lie without causing pain. Every sin we commit, however personal it seems, brings heartbreak, not only to ourselves, but to those about us. And if we "sow the wind, we will reap the whirlwind," not only personally, but in our society. Simple economics tells us why.

In Howard Ruff's book about the coming crunch, perhaps the most redeeming chapter is that on "Sin-Tax." Here he explains, "loosening sexual morality always ends up hitting society in the pocketbook. The exponential growth of welfare costs and property taxes can be directly traced to the sexual revolution, and it is the major contributing factor to juvenile crime, alcoholism, abortions, drug addiction, and disrupted schools that can no longer teach, but can only 'police,' and badly too. And you pay for it."

Ruff then goes on to say that now over half of the newborn black babies are illegitimate. Lest we think the problem is ethnic in origin, the illegitimacy rate for whites has doubled in the last ten years. Peter Schuck, deputy assistant secretary of Health, Education and Welfare, notes, "There is definitely a high correlation between out-of-wedlock births, welfare costs and many of our most pressing problems."

We are told statistically that only half of the unwed mothers in the United States ever hold even a part-time job during the first four years of their child's life. We are also told that nine out of ten of these women and children end up on welfare rolls costing taxpayers nearly $12 million in aid annually. The Urban Institute in Washington D.C. says that these unwed women cost us about $6 billion per year in welfare payments.

In addition to this staggering concern we also know that there is a growing epidemic of juvenile crime resulting from the lack of parental models in the homes. Because of the increased divorce rate 45 percent of today's children will grow up without one parent. As one psychologist says, "These people are going to put a growing burden on our society, not only to sustain them but to repair the social and economic damage they do." Understanding this, Ruff asserts, "I have long been convinced that the religious restrictions against extra-marital sex or pre-marital sex, which are common to the Christian and Hebrew Scriptures, are more for the protection of society than for the regulation of the life of the individual."

Although it is impossible to determine the exact amount sin costs each one of us in extra taxes, we do know it is more than $5 per day per family. These taxes are used to provide welfare benefits, fight juvenile crime, and to help curb the devastating effects of drug abuse, alcoholism, and crime. In addition there are staggering millions of dollars tacked onto our insurance premiums and the cost of merchandise and services because of thievery, fraudulent use of credit cards, and unscrupulous law-suits for unmerited malpractice and vandalism.

We Cannot Afford the High Cost of Sin

The only answers the psychologist, psychiatrist and politician seem to give us are more programs for more welfare recipients and their growing problems. Yet, it is clear that this does not work. Just one example of what happened in South Bronx, New York, should serve to remind us that more welfare is not the answer.

South Bronx is a city of over 500,000 people. The deterioration of the community started as much as thirty-five years ago and since that time the town has virtually become a welfare state. Today over 30 percent of the inhabitants are on welfare. The majority of the people have no fathers in their homes to provide stability and guidance. Half of the children drop out of school each year, and there is a whopping 60 percent unemployment rate.

Some eighty-nine organized gangs roam the streets mugging, raping, looting and murdering. Assaults are up 420 percent in the last ten years. Burglaries have jumped 700 percent. Tenement houses have deteriorated and crime control is virtually impossible.

Some time ago a few "bright" politicians decided that what was needed in areas like South Bronx was more welfare benefits, but this merely bred additional problems. One case in point: Welfare does not provide money for moving from one apartment to another unless the family has been burned out — so, the politicians provided a clause saying $1,000 to $3,000 would be given to any family who had been forced to move because of a fire. As a result the city of South Bronx has virtually been turned into an incinerator. In the last seven years there have been over 95,000 fires; more than thirty-three each night. It has been determined that over a third of the blazes have been deliberately set. Probably the number is far greater since arson is the hardest of all crimes to solve. And there is no hope in sight.

The Answer Is Not More Money, but Morality

Clearly the cure is not more money or welfare programs, but morality. Sin always has a high price tag to it and ends up hitting us all in the pocketbook. But, let us bring the problem down to an even more personal level. Here is how sin creates financial crises in our own homes.

All sin breaks the relationship between God and man, and between man and man. For example, sexual infidelity in a marriage creates family tensions and rivalry. Instability results in an effort to "get even" or cover the hurt. More mistakes are made. Husbands, driven by guilt, often load their wives or children with "guilt gifts" they can ill afford. These gifts do little to erase the pressure over the long haul and actually bring resentment. They can also mount up to create pressing financial burdens later on. Betrayed wives will often turn to material things to take their minds off their problems. They may charge new dresses, insist on bigger and nicer homes, or buy new furniture. Husbands may try to escape loneliness with new cars, boats or motorcycles. These obligations drive couples deeper in debt and into greater problems.

Psychologists tell us that the number one cause for divorce is money. However, now many of them are seeing that financial trouble is an effect, not a cause. In all my years of counseling I have never seen a couple in trouble without it affecting their finances. And very often when a couple starts having marital problems they can seldom afford the high-priced marriage counselors recommended to them by their friends. Usually, the more tense the relationship, the bleaker the couple's financial picture.

There is another way that financial disaster results from sin. Sensual pleasures are never sated, only teased. Graham Kerr, the "Galloping Gourmet," puts it this way: "When I tried to stuff the God-shaped void in my heart with 'things' the hole only got larger." Sin cannot be sated. It always takes more liquor and drugs for the next high than for the last. There is always the "next affair" that promises to be satisfying and the "next roll of the dice" that will bring fortune. Sadly it never does, but our sensual fantasies keep growing like Topsy until financial disaster strikes us down.

In addition to this, sin creates very real emotional and physical illnesses. It robs us of sleep and rest. There is little feeling of well-being when we are suffering from guilt or fear of discovery. That is why the Bible says, *But the wicked are like the troubled sea, when it cannot rest, whose waters cast up mire and dirt. There is no peace, saith my God, to the wicked* (Isaiah 57:20, 21). To still some restless hearts there must be drugs, escapism, and alcohol — more parties, more useless things bought to take the edge off unhappiness. All this costs money and creates financial havoc.

There Is an Answer

God never gives a craving without providing that which will satisfy it. There is water for the thirsty, food for the hungry, and love for the emotionally starved. And, there is an answer to the sin problem which creates financial havoc in our homes and in our land. Isaiah invites, *Ho, every one that thirsteth, come ye to the waters, and he that hath no money; come ye, buy, and eat; yea, come, buy wine and milk without money and without price. Wherefore do ye spend money for that which is not bread? And your labour for that which satisfieth not? hearken diligently unto me, and eat ye that which is good, and let your soul delight itself in fatness. Incline your ear, and come unto me: hear, and your soul shall live* (Isaiah 55:1-3).

God can come into our sorrows and bring help and healing. When we turn to Him many things begin to happen. The psalmist tells us of three: *Then shall the earth yield her increase; and God, even our own God, shall bless us. God shall bless us; and all the ends of the earth shall fear him* (Psalm 67:6, 7).

Note the three things that begin to happen: First, our physical world gets better. Second, God opens the windows of Heaven to us. And third, the rest of the world begins to see it really does pay to serve God.

Our Physical World Gets Better

When we turn to God our immediate world gets better. Our nerves are less frayed. We have the tension of sin drained from us. We sleep better. Our resources are not drained by debilitating habits. Our relationships with our family and friends greatly improve because we are at peace with God and ourselves.

Perhaps this is what Isaiah meant when he said, *And they shall beat their swords into plowshares, and their spears into pruning-hooks: nation shall not lift up sword against nation, neither shall they learn war any more* (Isaiah 2:4).

When we come to Christ all our defense mechanisms are changed to powerful and positive action. Rather than giving our lives to "getting even" and "doing our own thing" we now give ourselves to things that please God and bring love and health to our relationships. Our physical world does indeed become better and we are less defensive. Consequently, we are less uptight. The sun shines for us. Food tastes better. Music sounds more melodious and joy comes into our lives.

Blessings Are Tied to Obedience

When we turn to God He opens the windows of Heaven to bless us. He delights in giving us good things, just as an earthly father enjoys blessing his own children. The only thing that limits His blessings is our disobedience. If our child hurls a brick through a plate glass window, we cannot reward him for that gesture, but, if he is obedient and well mannered we thoroughly enjoy blessing him. So it is with our Heavenly Father. Our obedient lives unlock His treasure chest of Heaven to make us recipients of His great and good love gifts.

The World Sees

The greatest missionary impact we can make in our world is through our own lives. Our love touches the hearts of men more than our words. With the softening of our lives through the love of our Lord, people see the Christ within us and want to follow Him. Time and again I have seen this principle work. Graham Kerr was led to the Lord because he saw such a dramatic change in his wife's life after her conversion. He saw for the first time a tenderness in her. He wanted to give his heart to God, and his prayer for salvation was, "Lord, I don't understand what has happened to Treena, but whatever she has, I want."

Henry Drummond notes, "We measure great movements by the loudness of their advertisement, or the place their externals fill in the public eye. Christ's Kingdom has no externals. The usual methods of propagating a great cause were entirely discarded by Christ. The sword He declined; money He had none; literature he never used; the Church disowned Him; the State crucified Him. Planting His ideals in the hearts of a few poor men, He started them out unheralded to revolutionize the world. They did it by making friends — and by making enemies; they went about, did good, sowed seed, died, and lived again in the lives of those they helped." The world sees and wants what is in our hearts.

Sin costs, but there is an antidote to the sickness. We do not need to continue to be financially bound by evil. We can be free and grow in financial stability. However, before growth can come it is important that we understand clearly *the biggest barrier to financial success.*

5

The Biggest Barrier to Financial Success

Late in 1927 James Weldon Johnson captured the pathos and passion of the southern black preacher in his classic collection *God's Trombones.*[1] Although "The Creation" and "Go Down Death" are the most famous, and still performed on stage, it is the sermon-poem, "The Prodigal" which is most poignant.

Writing in the style of an old plantation preacher speaking to his congregation, Johnson starts this powerful poem with a lashing charge:

> *Young man! Young man! Your arms are too short to box with God.*

The brilliant statesman-poet was right; we can never fight with God and win. That is why any study of prosperity must start and end with man's relationship with his Creator. It is true that it is possible to amass great fortunes and possessions apart from God. However, true prosperity is far more than wealth — it is an inner rightness that affects all of our lives. Who among us has not seen people of great personal wealth still terribly unhappy? Prosperity therefore is not measured by the size of a savings account, but rather by the quality of a life.

Financial blessings may be part of prosperity, but certainly

1. James Weldon Johnson, *God's Trombones.* (New York: Viking, 1927).

not the whole. Yet the Bible does say there are certain things that will dry up our income and drain our financial resources. Recognizing these barriers to financial success will help us avoid fiscal disaster and improve our resources. Seven barriers to financial stability are listed. They are disobedience, misplaced values, indolence, parsimony, wanton pleasure, excessive appetites, and bad friends. All these will be discussed in later chapters, but it is interesting to note that at the top of the list is disobedience. From that seed of sin all the other weeds grow. We will find that while the word "disobedience" is a broad term, it is yet very specific.

To understand why disobedience is so devastating, we must remember that man was created for a specific purpose. Isaiah notes, *for I have created him for my glory, I have formed him; yea, I have made him* (Isaiah 43:7). Add to this Paul's words on several occasions, *That we should be to the praise of his glory* (Ephesians 1:12). We were made to bring glory to our Creator and to live in relationship with Him. When we rebel against that purpose we circumvent God's divine plan and lock up the treasury of Heaven.

We have seen that our disobedience to God's intended purpose brings poverty to ourselves and to others about us — not only in the area of finance, but also in bankrupted relationships. It is imperative we understand this. In fact, the quality of our relationships to others is directly related to our distance to or from our Creator. Perhaps this point was most dramatically made in the following story of a famous family who learned the lesson too late.

Relationships Are Not Disposable

One of the saddest books I have read in the last decade is *Haywire*,[2] the tragic story of the Hayward family. Written by daughter Brooke Hayward, the book traces the fortunes and follies of Leland Hayward, Hollywood producer-agent, his actress wife Margaret Sullavan, and their three brilliant and beautiful children. They had the potential of being an

---

2. Brooke Hayward, *Haywire*. (New York: Alfred Knopf, 1977).

ideal family. But the book tells how Leland married five times without ever really finding happiness. Margaret, with no sure foundation to her life, married four times and finally killed herself. Then the three children's heartbreaks are bared. The only boy, Bill, struggled with deep emotional problems and was confined in a mental institution on several occasions. Brooke suffered a harsh divorce and had to grapple with problems of personal adjustments and fears. Bridgette, the younger sister, killed herself in a period of despondency. She was beautiful and vivacious, but snuffed out her life while barely past her teens.

Perhaps one of the most moving scenes of the whole book is captured in the last pages. The years have flown. The family has long ago broken up. The mother and one daughter are dead by their own hands. Leland lies dying on a hospital bed. Brooke and her tormented brother sit by the lonely bedside thinking of all the wasted years. Finally after hours of suffering Leland dies, and Brooke writes through her tears:

"I wept for my family, all of us, my beautiful idyllic lost family. I wept for our excesses, our delusions and inconsistencies, not that we had cared too much or too little, although both were true, but that we had let such extraordinary care be subverted into such extraordinary carelessness. We'd been careless with the best of our many resources: each other. It is as if we'd taken for granted the fact that, like our talents and interests and riches, there would be more where we had come from too; another chance, another summer, another Brooke or Bridgette or Bill."

Having no stable relationship with the Creator, the Haywards could not manage a stable relationship with each other. They learned too late that relationships are not disposable.

Long ago the prophet Malachi dealt with this problem, and in the Bible he tells us that a broken relationship with God will bankrupt us spiritually, emotionally, physically and financially. He says, *If ye will not hear, and if ye will not lay it to heart, to give glory unto my name, saith the Lord of hosts, I will even send a curse upon you, and I will curse your blessings: yea, I have cursed them already, because ye do not lay it to heart* (Malachi 2:2).

Malachi wants to make sure Israel understands exactly what charges of disobedience God brings against them. Thus he lists four blatant acts of rebellion they committed. First of all they prostituted God's Word. Their prayers of repentance were not sincere. They dealt treacherously in their relationships with each other. And finally, they justified their acts of disobedience to themselves and to God.

Malachi's charges have a strong resemblance to sins of our age. Therefore, they could and should be considered with profit. First the angry prophet says Israel profaned God's Word by mixing it with other world philosophies; they *married the daughter of a strange God* (Malachi 2:11). This simply means they had turned wine into water. Rather than obeying God's Word, they mixed His commandments with their own ideas and the concepts of pagan religions. Thus, they made His Word of no effect. In our age of "doing our own thing" and doing whatever feels good to us, we make the same dreadful mistake. And, this disobedience can bankrupt us.

The second charge was that Israel's tears of repentance were not real. They prayed, but it was not for forgiveness of sin; rather it was to escape the consequences of their deeds. They wanted to dance but did not want to pay the piper.

One preacher wisely said, "Most of us sow our wild oats and then pray for a crop failure." Unfortunately, it doesn't work that way. Paul talks of the two kinds of sorrow, *For Godly sorrow worketh repentance to salvation not to be repented of: but the sorrow of the world worketh death* (II Corinthians 7:10).

Most of us have seen alcoholics who have not wanted to be made whole — only sober. There are philanderers who want release from the consequences of their unfaithfulness; but do not want to give up their lifestyle. This was the case of disobedient Israel. The people wanted to be free from the consequences — but to continue the evil. Because of this act of open disobedience they slammed shut God's treasure house of blessing to them.

Probably the third charge against Israel brought more family pain than any other sin they committed. Malachi said they dealt treacherously in their family relationships. When they tired of a marriage they abandoned it, rather than work through it. The people practiced conditional love; as long as their mates pleased them they stayed together. But, when other more attractive persons captured their fancy they left their marriages to follow their passions. They lived as though love was a feeling rather than a responsibility.

Perhaps this last sin is the most blatant act of disobedience committed in our day. Divorce rates are soaring. Through television, radio, song, novel, and drama we are told daily that love is a feeling.

Johnny Cash's country song epitomizes our fickle attitude toward love's relationships:

We got married in a fever
Hotter than a Pepper Sprout.
But we've been thinkin' about Jackson
Ever since the fire went out.

God's Word says such an attitude is disobedience and will bankrupt us. Clearly God calls us to a responsibility that overshadows our fickle feelings. Paul outlines this in the Bible's great love chapter (I Corinthians 13). We are not to abandon a relationship of promise just because our feelings change.

Finally, the people of Israel justified their actions (Malachi 2:17) and this was counted as an act of disobedience to God. It is true that almost any of our actions can be justified in our own eyes, but the final judgment is not one of circumstances or feeling. Rather it is the Word of God. We must never forget there is a fixed star in our universe by which we guide the ship of our lives. We must obey God, since one day we will stand before Him and give an account of deeds done in the flesh.

Their Disobedience Brought Financial Ruin

Sin affected the pocketbooks of Israel, and the people experienced personal poverty of spirit and resources. This is why the Bible says, *Fools because of their transgression, and because of their iniquities, are afflicted* (Psalm 107:17). Again, *Therefore I will wound you! I will make your hearts miserable for all your sins. You will eat but never have enough; hunger pangs and emptiness will still remain. And though you try and try to save your money, it will come to nothing at the end, and what little you succeed in storing up I'll give to those who conquer you! You will plant crops but not harvest them; you will press out the oil from the olives, and not get enough to anoint yourself! You will trample the grapes, but get no juice to make your wine* (Micah 6:13-15, Living Bible).

Although it is clear that our prosperity is directly tied to our obedience to God we often ask, "Why do the wicked seem to prosper?" It is a legitimate question pondered long ago by greater men with greater minds than ours. But, again the Bible has the answer. The psalmist says, *Yet it is so hard to explain it — this prosperity of those who hate the Lord. Then one day I went into God's sanctuary to meditate, and thought about the future of these evil men. What a slippery path they are on — suddenly God will send them sliding over the edge of the cliff and down to their destruction: an instant end to all their happiness, an eternity of terror. Their present life is only a dream! They will awaken to the truth as one awakens from a dream of things that never really were!* (Psalm 73:16-21, Living Bible).

The seeming prosperity of the wicked is only an illusion. It will never last and that is why we must never fix our attention on it.

Permanent Prosperity Is God's Gift

Prosperity is directly linked to our relationship with God, and our relationship to God affects all other life relationships.

Moses carefully prepared the people for what would happen to them if they deliberately disobeyed their God. In a most striking chapter, (Leviticus 25) he traces the progression of sufferings that come because of sinful disobedience. Moses tells Israel that problems will get progressively worse until repentance is realized. He said at first, because of disobedience they could expect fear, sickness, and poverty. Then, if they still did not repent, would come servitude, drought, and accidents to their children. If they continued to thumb their noses at God there would come war, want, starvation, death; their possessions given to their enemies and their children scattered among the heathen. The cost of sin is horribly high.

But Moses notes there is a day as well as a night. If the people will obey God, he says God will sign a contract with them. *If you obey all of my commandments, I will give you regular rains, and the land will yield bumper crops, and the trees will be loaded with fruit long after the normal time! And grapes will be ripening when sowing time comes again. You shall eat your fill, and live safely in the land, for I will give you peace, and you will go to sleep without fear.*

He continues, quoting God: *I will chase away the dangerous animals. You will chase your enemies. . . . I will look after you and multiply you, and fulfill my covenant with you. You will have such a surplus of crops that you won't know what to do with them when the new harvest is ready! And I will live among you, and not despise you. I will walk among you and be your God, and you shall be my people. For I am the Lord your God who brought you out of the land of Egypt, with the intention that you be slaves no longer; I have broken your chains and will make you walk with dignity* (Leviticus 26:3-13, Living Bible).

The key to prosperity is obedience. But, we must keep in mind God said, "If you obey *all* my commandments." We cannot choose the ones we wish to obey and ignore the rest. His Word is not a cafeteria from which we choose the desserts most appealing to us. Rather, His Word is a prescription that must be taken in its entirety if health, healing and prosperity are to follow.

6

Three Things that Devour Your Dollars

One positive result of the energy crisis has been a new awareness of the need to conserve our resources. Realizing we have only so many resources available, utility companies, oil corporations, and consumer affairs advocates are issuing a whole series of books and pamphlets on how to save fuel, and consequently money.

They tell us that each heating degree above 68 Fahrenheit and cooling degree below 75 costs us an additional five percent per degree on our utility bill. Driving our cars above 55 miles per hour adds a proportionate percentage to our fuel consumption. We are given all kinds of advice on lighting for less, cutting cooking costs, trimming cleaning bills, and generally stopping the drain of our dollars in wasteful ways.

All this advice is excellent, and it is true that we in the western world usually throw away more than most people live on. But, the Bible gives even more basic and better advice on how to conserve our dollars. Three villains the Bible exposes are misplaced values, indolence, and parsimony.

Heading the list is "misplaced values." And it should, since this problem creates emotional and financial bankruptcy.

The Millionaire Pauper

Hetty Green of Massachusetts inherited a small fortune from

her father in 1835. Through shrewd management she parlayed the money to over $100 million and became known as "the wizard of Wall Street." Yet for all her riches, Hetty Green lived like a pauper. When one of her children broke his leg, Hetty did not call a doctor — the expense was too great, she felt — and instead took him to a charity hospital, where she passed herself off as a beggar.

Unfortunately the condition of young Edward Green's leg grew worse and amputation was necessary if his life were to be saved. Hetty had the operation performed in her rooming house, to save the fee at the hospital. In later years Hetty lived in an unheated tenement and subsisted on a diet of cold eggs and onions, to spare the cost of heating her food. She wore newspapers for underwear, and allowed only the lower half of her petticoat to be laundered. At her death in 1916 Hetty Green left $125 million to her heirs.

While Hetty had money, she certainly did not have prosperity. She was spiritually and emotionally bankrupt because misplaced values had distorted her thinking and blocked God's blessings. Haggai told us all about this.

Called to bring Israel back to the God-assigned task of building the Temple, Haggai rails, *Is it then the right time for you to live in luxurious homes, when the Temple lives in ruins? Look at the result: You plant much but harvest little. You have scarcely enough to eat or drink, and not enough clothes to keep you warm. Your income disappears, as though you were putting it into pockets filled with holes! "Think it over," says the Lord of Hosts. "Consider how you have acted, and what has happened as a result!"* (Haggai 1:3-7, Living Bible).

Continuing his angry charge Haggai moves on. *You hope for much but get so little. And when you bring it home, I blow it away — it doesn't last at all. Why? Because my Temple lies in ruins and you don't care. Your only concern is your own fine homes. That is why I am holding back the rains from heaven and giving you such scant crops. In fact I have called for a drought upon the land, yes, and in the highlands, too; a drought to wither the grain and grapes and olives and all your other crops, a drought to starve both you and your cattle, and ruin everything you have worked so hard to get* (Haggai 1:9-11, Living Bible).

The cry is clear. We have been called to a great task of being involved with God in redeeming mankind. But, if we get preoccupied with our own pleasures and possessions, He will take drastic measures against us. The world is hurting too deeply for us to play around with building bigger barns and losing ourselves in the lust and greed of our age.

Our Lord knows we have certain needs. He wants us to prosper. But He warns: *You cannot serve two masters: God and money. For you will hate one and love the other, or else the other way around.*

So my counsel is: Don't worry about things — food, drink, and clothes. For you already have life and a body — and they are far more important than what to eat and wear. Look at the birds! They don't need to sow or reap or store up food — for your heavenly Father feeds them. And you are far more valuable to him than they are. Will all your worries add a single moment to your life?

And why worry about your clothes? Jesus continues, *Look at the field lilies! They don't worry about theirs. Yet King Solomon in all his glory was not clothed as beautifully as they.*

And if God cares so wonderfully for flowers that are here today and gone tomorrow, won't he more surely care for you, O men of little faith?

So don't worry at all about having enough food and clothing. Why be like the heathen? For they take pride in all these things and are deeply concerned about them. But your heavenly Father already knows perfectly well that you need them, and he will give them to you if you give him first place in your life and live as He wants you to.

So don't be anxious about tomorrow. God will take care of your tomorrow too. Live one day at a time (Matthew 6:24-34, Living Bible).

Thus, misplaced values block our blessings from God. Why should He give us any more resources if we have not properly used the ones He has already given to us? The world is in too much want for any of us to waste.

One of the saddest statements in the Bible is made about the prodigal son. Jesus says, *and there wasted his substance with riotous living* (Luke 15:13).

I agree with Billy Graham. God indeed will have to make an apology to Sodom and Gomorrah if He fails to bring judgment on our western world which has so much and shares so little.

It is hard for me to understand how we can buy bigger and better boats, have motorcycles scattered around like toys, drive finer and newer cars, put up greater and more costly mansions — yet complain because we are called on to give more to missions. God forgive us if we continue to "waste our substance on riotous living." There will come a day of want when we "fain to fill our belly with the husk of hogs." God has given us great resources and the privilege and responsibility of channeling these into His work.

Parsimony

Parsimony is simply "stinginess." And it will bankrupt us. Perhaps Daniel Dancer was the world's worst miser. In the annals of miserdom, no account is more pitiable than that of Daniel Dancer and his sister, who lived and died in eighteenth-century England. Daniel, however, was the stingier of the two, for in the worship of mammon, he sacrificed his sister's life.

Lying on the heap of rags that was her bed, the dying Miss Dancer worsened from day to day yet received no medical attention. When asked why he did not call a doctor for his sister, Daniel replied, "Why should I waste my money in wickedly endeavouring to counteract the will of Providence?"

All the while his sister lay ill Daniel made no change in her customary diet of one cold dumpling and a strip of fatty meat. When she objected that so meager a supper was not enough for one who was sick, Daniel told her, "If you don't like it, you may go without it."

The Dancer siblings were by no means poor: they had an annual income of £3,000 a year from their farmlands in Harrow, just south of London. Yet they were so frugal that on one occasion, while walking on their grounds, they came upon the rotting carcass of a sheep that had obviously died of disease. They skinned this decaying hulk, and made meat pies with what little flesh remained.

Daniel would obtain fertilizer for his fields by walking along the common road, stuffing his pockets with the cow dung he found there. While he had his nose to the ground for manure, he also foraged for old bones: what meat was on the bones would go toward his dinner.

There is little to admire about a miser. He not only makes himself miserable but his misery affects others. The Bible talks about such people by saying, *It is possible to give away and become richer! It is also possible to hold on too tightly and lose everything. Yes, the liberal man shall be rich! By watering others, he waters himself* (Proverbs 11:24, 25, Living Bible).

From the beginning God has instituted the law of seed times and harvest. If we do not sow, we will not reap. Thus, a man who hoards his resources plants no seed and gets no harvest. But the generous man plants seeds all around, and God opens up the windows of Heaven to bless him. This is why Jesus said, *For if you give, you will get! Your gift will return to you in full and overflowing measure, pressed down, shaken together to make room for more, and running over. Whatever measure you use to give — large or small — will be used to measure what is given back to you* (Luke 6:38, Living Bible).

Tied closely to parsimony is the present trend of hoarding now sweeping the western world. Commenting on this recent wave, one cartoonist depicted a wife talking with her husband: "I wonder if we shouldn't start hoarding things before it becomes unpatriotic again."

Time magazine recently commented on the trend saying:

> Some commentators on American behavior think that today's sporadic hoarding of gasoline is an isolated phenomenon unlikely to spread to other products. Says Sociologist Amitai Etzioni: "People have a very emotional stake in their cars. It's not rational and subject to the usual calculations." But others view it more seriously. Says Harvard Historian Frank Freidel: "Hoarding is an absolutely typical American trait."
>
> Some social scientists warn of a "shortage psychosis" and see the jittery outbreaks of minor hoarding during the '70s —

runs on saccharin, beef, coffee and canning lids — as a sign of a major problem ahead. If uncertainty is allowed to continue then people are really likely to do panicky things.

One lesson learned during World War II is that hoarding of one item can cause a run on another. In 1943 the rationing of shoes touched of hoarding of clothes, and the rationing of canned meats and fish started panic buying of canned vegetables and fruit. Another lesson is that scarcity is not essential to hoarding. In 1973, reporting a Congressman's fatuous remark that supplies might grow short, TV Host Johnny Carson touched off nationwide panic buying of toilet paper.

One key ingredient in all hoarding is distrust. "The ordinary human being knows that Government authorities and business leaders give a lot higher priority to keeping the populace calm than to telling the truth," one sociologist says.

Factors other than a loss of faith in government may also be at work: a competitive culture, high anxiety about the economy and conflicting reports on which shortages are long-term or temporary. Sociologist Jackie Boles says, "At times like this we need strong leadership to jolt people out of this competitive behavior. Unfortunately, our leadership has said, 'Yes, we have an energy shortage,' and 'No, we don't have an energy shortage.' People are operating in a vacuum of leadership. Another says, 'The public will try to get the facts themselves, and when no reliable facts are available, they will create their own drama.'"

We do know that lines are forming, and anyone reluctant to join may not get his share. Psychologist Philip Owens says, "If an individual sees a line, he's apt to get into it, even if he doesn't know what it's for." In such a climate, social pressures against overbuying disappear; and everyone can hoard in seeming good conscience. One refrain dates back to World War II: "I'm just stocking up before the hoarders get here."

Hoarding could become more severe than it was during the war. Says Princeton Historian Eric Goldman: "Rationing was resented then, but it was temporary; all we had to do was win the war. Today's nagging feeling about shortages comes from being helpless, (that) we aren't going to get out of this easily."

God's Word tells us we should not hoard. In fact, when Israel hoarded the manna it spoiled. The principle is clear — they should have lived in day-tight compartments trusting God, not material things. The Scripture still says, *There is that scattereth, and yet increaseth; and there is that withholdeth more than is meet, but it tendeth to poverty* (Proverbs 11:24).

Indolence

One of the first laws of business is, "There ain't no such thing as a free lunch." While not said in the same vernacular, still the principle of God's Word is the same. God intends that we *work* on the spaceship called earth. We are not to lie around waiting for the world to pay our bills. God has never, nor will He ever condone laziness.

Paul says frankly, *Even while we were still there with you we gave you this rule: "He who does not work shall not eat."*

Yet we hear, Paul goes on to add, *that some of you are living in laziness, refusing to work, and wasting your time in gossiping. In the name of the Lord Jesus Christ we appeal to such people — we command them — to quiet down, get to work, and earn their own living* (II Thessalonians 3:10, 11, Living Bible).

Work was never the curse of sin. Rather, it was the toil involved with work that came as a result of man's disobedience. Long before man sinned God placed him in the garden and gave him a work assignment. Also, we know that in Heaven we will work, *his servants shall serve him* (Revelation 22:3). And the Bible says laziness and refusal to work is a form of disobedience to God. Therefore it will bring us to poverty.

There are a number of Proverbs addressing indolence. Note this one: *Lazy people want much but get little, while the diligent are prospering* (Proverbs 13:4, Living Bible). Again, *Lazy men are soon poor; hard workers get rich. A wise youth makes hay while the sun shines, but what a shame to see a lad who sleeps away his hour of opportunity* (Proverbs 10:4, 5, Living Bible).

And once more, *A lazy man is brother to the saboteur* (Proverbs 18:9, Living Bible).

There is no question about our facing very real problems in our society because of indolence. The welfare roles are growing greater while more of our people refuse to work. Our social security system is threatened with bankruptcy sometime in the future because of this. There used to be ninety workers in the United States supporting each person in the Social Security program. Now there are three. Fifteen years from now (if the system is still functioning by then), there will only be two. Our whole nation is threatened with poverty because of indolence. This shouldn't surprise us since the Bible said it would be so.

Not only do misplaced values, stinginess, and laziness drain our dollars, but there is another terrible trio that nibble away at them until we have little left. They are excessive appetites, wanton pleasure, and bad friends.

7

Another Trio that Devaluates Your Dollars

Two young boys were whiling away a lazy summer afternoon making extravagant wishes when one mused, "I wish I had a million dollars."

"What would you do with a million dollars?" the other asked.

"Why, I'd pay my bills as far as it would go," the first youth said innocently.

Probably many of us know how the boy felt. At times our financial obligations get so burdensome it feels as though we personally owe the national debt. Sometimes we have the same sensation as bailing water out of a sinking boat. Many give up and declare bankruptcy; the rate of those dodging legitimate obligations through bankruptcy has sharply escalated in recent years.

It is very true that the borrower is servant to the lender, and our financial obligations can keep us from enjoying many of the blessings of our heavenly Father. In a later chapter we will deal with the problem of debts. Yet, diagnosis is not cure. There must be more than merely articulating the problem to arrive at a solution. This is where the Bible shines. God's Word is therapy predicated on the principle that it is better to build a fence at the top of the hill than a hospital at the bottom. Therefore, the Bible clearly warns us about the things that will devaluate our dollars and get us into a financial quagmire.

Wanton Pleasure

One day a pastor called on a family in his congregation. When he knocked on the door the ten-year-old son answered.

"Hi, is your daddy home?" the pastor asked.

"Nope, he's playing golf," the boy offered.

"Well, is your mother home?"

"Nah, she's over to her friend's house playing bridge."

"What about your sister?" the pastor persisted.

"Look, mister," the impatient boy blurted out, "She's out on a date and I wouldn't be here either except I've got a tomcat in the freezer trying to turn him into a polar bear."

The boy was certainly keeping himself occupied although we would rightly question just how healthy his diversion was, especially for the tomcat. But it seems as though our whole western world is spending itself in contrived distractions and diversions. Perhaps there has been no culture since Noah's day that is more devoted to seeking pleasure than our own. Travel trailers crawl over millions of miles of our highways each year, followed by cars and trucks towing massive boats, motorcycles, and smaller trailers. Huge pleasure palaces such as those in Las Vegas, Reno and Atlantic City dot our landscape. The sporting goods and entertainment industries are like giant kingdoms controlling much of our wealth. Many reasonable people are becoming increasingly worried about today's preoccupation with pleasure.

Perhaps in such a time it would be well to note what God's Word has to say. The proverbist warns, *A man who loves pleasure becomes poor; wine and luxury are not the way to riches!"* (Proverbs 21:17, Living Bible). And if we refuse to heed this word from the Lord we must take note, *Poverty and shame shall be to him that refuseth instruction: but he that regardeth reproof shall be honoured* (Proverbs 13:18).

Although the message is not pleasant, it is still true. And not only does the preacher proclaim it, but those who have the responsibility of governing our land know that wanton pleasure will bring us to poverty. Long ago John Adams wisely noted, "Our constitution was made for only a moral and religious people. It is wholly inadequate to the government of any other."

Add to this the wise words of Edmund Burke, "Men of intemperate habits cannot be free. Their passions form their fetter."

We have already considered the dire consequences of infidelity. Not only is there great emotional upheaval and pain for all involved, but dollars are drained away from family incomes. Think then of the enormous losses at race tracks, gambling halls, and in bars. To our shame the alcoholic has become a national cliché and millions of dollars and talents are wasted through this escape into sensual pleasure.

Not long ago James Reston wrote a frightening column about the coming food shortage in our world. One especially heart-sickening statement he made was, "While the average person in poor countries consumes about 400 pounds of grain a year, the average North American is now consuming nearly a ton of grain a year, about 100 pounds of it in the form of beer and whiskey." He then went on to add, "The guess here is that the United States could make more friends and progress in the world by solving the food crisis than by fiddling with the missile crisis. But this will take some doing. The rich world doesn't really believe in the coming food crisis any more than it believes in the oil crisis, but it will. One day we all will be weight watchers."

It is to our shame that Americans drink up over a quarter of what half of the world survives on annually. Certainly God must bring us to judgment for this.

Drunkenness and Gluttony

North America controls a larger share of the world's exportable food grains than the Middle East does of oil. This statement raises some deep moral questions. As Lester Brown of the Overseas Development Council asks, "Can we rely primarily on the marketplace to set the price and determine the distribution of so essential a commodity as food? And should Americans continue to consume as much fodder as they do now? Most of us consume more than we actually need."

The question is a hard one — especially during the present oil crisis. Some politicians are demanding that the price of a bushel of wheat be determined by the price of oil. But is this really a righteous question when the nations that need the food most are those who are least able to pay for it? Brown says, "There is little doubt that a major food crisis is developing now in Asia and we will have to decide whether to cut Asia adrift and let thousands die, or give up some of our gluttony so grain can be freed to go there."

World demand for food, because of rising populations, is increasing by thirty million tons a year. In 1961 we had food reserves for ninety-five days of world consumption. Now, despite very good crops in the major grain-producing countries, reserves are down to twenty-seven days and declining at the alarming rate of ten tons per year. This prompted Reston to add, "The United States farmers and the Department of Agriculture are as great a contribution to world peace as the soldiers at the Pentagon or the diplomats at the State Department."

Again in the face of these alarming statistics we need to look at God's Word and find perspective as followers of Jesus Christ. The Bible says, *For the drunkard and the glutton shall come to poverty: and drowsiness shall clothe a man with rags* (Proverbs 23:21). Again it is well to remember that in ancient Israel the punishment for drunkenness and gluttony, along with rebellion, was death. (Deuteronomy 21:20,21).

It is no accident, I believe, that God has blessed our nation with the abundance we have. The United States and Canada are not withholding grain from hungry nations for political or economic purposes. I don't think it due to freak circumstances we have what we have. Rather God has given this "Christian" world the resources, so we may give to others. We are the world's supply line. God forbid that we should shut up our hearts of mercy to a waiting and wanting world. That is what John meant when he said, *But if someone who is supposed to be a Christian has money enough to live well, and sees a brother in need, and won't help him — how can God's love be within him? Little children, let us stop just saying we love people; let us really love them and show it by our actions* (I John 3:17, 18, Living Bible).

Remembering that financial blessings come from God as a

direct result of our obedience, it is easy to understand that hoarding for ourselves will bring poverty. Again we are reminded that we are channels of blessings, not reservoirs of resources. This concept is hard for us to grasp at times, but it is still true.

Paul said, *Of course, I don't mean that those who receive your gifts should have an easy time of it at your expense, but you should divide with them. Right now you have plenty and can help them; then at some other time they can share with you when you need it. In this way each will have as much as he needs. Do you remember what the Scriptures say about this? "He that gathered much had nothing left over, and he that gathered little had enough!" So you also should share with those in need* (II Corinthians 8:13-15, Living Bible).

In the next few years we, as a nation, have critical choices before us. My prayer is that we will make the right decisions. If we do, the great blessings of our past will spill over into the future. However, if we continue to consume most of the earth's resources selfishly, then I believe God will shift these resources to a more responsible people, just as he shifted the message of salvation to the "new Israel." May it not be said of us, as it was of Israel, *But they also have erred through wine, and through strong drink are out of the way; the priest and the prophet have erred through strong drink, they are swallowed up of wine, they are out of the way through strong drink; they err in vision, they stumble in judgment* (Isaiah 28:7).

While we pray for our country and exert our personal influence for right decisions, we can have a more direct and effective influence right where we are. This can be in our attitude toward a wanting world. No longer can we give excuses that there is nothing we can do. There is plenty we can and should do. For one thing we can make a conscious effort to involve ourselves and our families in sacrificial giving to missions. Today there are excellent missionary organizations such as World Vision or Dr. Mark Buntain's feeding program in India that make it possible for us to answer a hungry world.

Dr. Buntain feeds eleven thousand starving children every day in Calcutta, India. He can do this for as little as ten cents per child per day. School children and churchmen from all over North

America are sending their dimes and dollars to feed these hungry children, so something can and is being done. But we must do more. Every family member should learn to give sacrificially for missions. Then, I believe, God will continue to bless our families and our resources. Standing together we can make an impact on our hungry world.

Bad Friends Waste Our Money

A decade ago the press assaulted our senses with the terrible atrocities perpetrated against the inmates of two Arkansas prisons. We were told of torture chambers, of beatings, and abuses. Newspapers front-paged devices of suffering such as the "Tucker telephone" and the beating strap. Yet, as a former prison chaplain in those institutions, I can truthfully say the greatest abuse of all is not physical, but emotional. Men can and have endured terrible physical abuse which we can never condone, but it is not the worst torture. The deepest hurt of all is the violence of loneliness, and the greatest punishment, "isolation." When a man is locked in a dark cell away from all human contact he is able to endure for a while but finally the loneliness breaks him down.

This should not surprise us since from the beginning the Bible says it is not good for man to be alone. We are created with not only a God-shaped void in our lives, but also a human-shaped void. We can only be really complete when we have a healthy relationship with God and with our fellow human beings. That is why friendship is so important. Even so, we must be careful what friends we chose. They will either make us or break us. The Bible tells us that.

Long ago God's Words warned about the influence of relationships: *He that walketh with wise men shall be wise: but a companion of fools shall be destroyed* (Proverbs 13:20).

Moses noted the power of friendship when he told Israel, *If thy brother, the son of thy mother, or thy son, or thy daughter, or the wife of thy bosom, or thy friend, which is as thine own soul, entice thee secretly, saying, Let us go and serve other gods, which thou hast not known, thou, nor thy father, Thou shalt not consent unto him, nor hearken unto him; neither shall thine eye pity him, neither shalt thou spare, neither shalt thou conceal him* (Deuteronomy 13:6,8). Then Moses dares to go on to advise such crime merits death! The point of the passage is to show how deeply we can be influenced to sin by those about us.

Henry Ford was once asked, "Who is your best friend?" The auto magnate replied, "The one who brings out the best in me." It was an excellent answer because we do have a tendency to become like those with whom we associate. The Bible says, *He that tilleth his land shall have plenty of bread: but he that followeth after vain persons shall have poverty enough* (Proverbs 28:19). Again, *Be not among winebibbers; among riotous eaters of flesh: For the drunkard and the glutton shall come to poverty* (Proverbs 23:20,21).

Because we have a tendency to become like those close to us Paul warns that we should not be *unequally yoked together with unbelievers* (II Corinthians 6:14). This yoke is a working relationship that has to do with our businesses, our marriages and our social lives. We must keep in mind that while Jesus was friendly with sinners, His closest friends were Peter, James, and John; Mary, Martha, and Lazarus. He clearly understood the power and purpose of friendship and chose His friends well.

Friends We Should Have

Obviously the first prerequisite for friendship is righteousness. Paul asks, *what do the people of God have in common with the people of sin? How can light live with darkness? And what harmony can there be between Christ and the devil? How can a Christian be a partner with one who doesn't believe?* (II Corinthians 6:14, 15, Living Bible).

Another prerequisite is that our friends should be spiritually stimulating. The Bible says, *A mirror reflects a man's face, but what he is really like is shown by the kind of friends he chooses* (Proverbs 27:19, Living Bible).

Then we are told, that the friends we choose should be emotionally stable: *Make no friendship with angry man; and with a furious man thou shalt not go: Lest thou learn his ways, and get a snare to thy soul* (Proverbs 22:24). It is true that unresolved anger creates most emotional problems and these spill over into life's relationships. We tend to reflect the attitudes and mannerisms of our friends, and by associating with emotionally sick people our own values can become terribly distorted.

The Bible also tells us what kind of friends we are to be, *A true friend is always loyal* (Proverbs 17:17, Living Bible), and *Faithful are the wounds of a friend; but the kisses of an enemy are deceitful* (Proverbs 27:6). Moving on, the proverbist adds, *Ointment and perfume rejoice the heart: so doth the sweetness of a man's friend by hearty counsel* (Proverbs 27:9).

In review we see the terrible trio that gobbles up our dollars — wanton pleasure, excessive appetites, and evil friends. Add to these the other terrible three: misplaced values, indolence, and parsimony, and we have a deadly concoction that will bankrupt us. All this is basic disobedience to God. And as we have already learned, disobedience locks up the treasures of God and cancels out His paychecks to us.

But, enough of the negative. What can we do to stretch our dollars? How can we bail out the sinking boat and keep the ship in trim so we might sail through rough financial waters unharmed? Well, again the Bible is not silent.

8

Five Income Stretchers

Within the last few years appreciable gains have been made in getting more out of less. Perhaps the most striking example is that of food production. Today, because of improved livestock, feeds and better medicines, a cow in the United States produces an average of 10,000 pounds of milk per year. Lest that fail to impress us, we must remember a cow in India is able to produce only about 600 pounds of milk annually.

This great increase in milk production does not satisfy the Department of Agriculture in Washington, however. They want to know why a cow in Washington state could produce 44,000 pounds of milk last year, and why the American hen, even when tricked by controlled lighting, produces only 232 eggs a year, while the Japanese actually induced one hen to lay 364! Our grain output is also improving with corn production now up four percent per acre. Soybeans growing at accelerated rates have virtually become a world staple with our exports bringing in more money than all the high technology exports such as computers and jet aircraft.

Experts, looking for a "conceptual breakthrough," are now trying to induce multiple births in feed animals. Some are even talking of cloning—to help still the gnawing hunger pangs of our expanding world. It seems as though all responsible people are getting involved in stretching resources and getting more out of less. It is an exciting and healthy concept, especially when we realize we haven't even tapped most of our earth's resources yet. God's Word tells us He has locked great treasures in our earth and it is the joy of man to uncover them. (Proverbs 25:2).

While man wrestles with nature to forfeit her secrets, God has already revealed great truths to those who follow Him. All we have to do is look and learn. The Bible says, *Surely the Lord God will do nothing, but he revealeth his secret unto his servants the prophets* (Amos 3:7). We can save a lot of time and wasted expense by looking into God's Word to discover very practical ways we can increase our income and stretch our dollars.

Look in the Right Direction

When we get into financial difficulty we all have a tendency to look to human organizations for help. We trust our social security system, savings accounts, credit unions, or caring relatives. Often the last recourse is the courts. However, God wants us to learn that He is really our only source. It seems to be a lesson we need to relearn daily. God has not hidden this from us. The Bible is crammed full of that concept in parable, example, direct statement and type. Note the Bible comments on the good reign of King Uzziah, *and as long as he sought the Lord, God made him to prosper* (II Chronicles 26:5).

Prosperity is directly from the hand of God. Therefore, when trouble comes we need to *look to the hills from whence cometh our help* (Psalm 121:1). Ultimately the union, the government, the bank, or the courts do not have the answer to our problems. Most often they only delay the solution or compound the difficulty. We must learn to lean on God at all times, good and bad.

Another very real problem that we have is looking for more in others than they can give. This is especially true of husbands and wives. Often because of shattering childhood experiences a wife will have an exaggerated need of security from her husband. Or a husband might have an exaggerated need of approval from his wife. Unless both come to grips with the difficulty it will create emotional and even financial bankruptcy. The reason is that when either mate looks to the other for more than the other can give, he is disappointed and damaged. Sometimes when those needs are not met, one party, or both, will start to look to someone else or something else for fulfillment. This is when possessions become security blankets and tools to escape the unhappiness of a relationship. Betty was a case in point.

Betty had a deep need for security — a need far deeper than her husband could cope with. He could never assure her enough so she tried to fill the need with possessions. She bought the "latest" clothes. She insisted on a new home although the old one was more than adequate. Finally she was engulfed in trying to juggle all the financial balls in the air and wondered why her relationship with her family was deteriorating. The marriage was already ruptured when she came to see me.

When Betty came for counseling I tried to gently lead her to an awareness of what she was doing. After a while she saw that her possessions — home, and material comforts — represented a degree of security for her that her husband could not supply. However, as always happens, Betty's possessions began to possess her, and her relationship with her husband came to the breaking point. Her husband gave up trying to fulfill her needs and sought a relationship elsewhere. In her distorted quest for security she lost the only thing she ever really wanted, a loving family.

It was at this time God helped us to softly lead Betty to the source of her needs. We told her that only God could give her real security, and in due course we helped her take the pressure off her harried husband.

We started by sharing Paul's admonition, *But godliness with contentment is great gain* (I Timothy 6:6). Again, *Stay away from the love of money; be satisfied with what you have. For God has said, "I will never, never fail you nor forsake you." That is why we can say without any doubt or fear, "The Lord is my Helper and I am not afraid of anything that mere man can do to me* (Hebrews 13:5, 6, Living Bible). John the Baptist had told the soldiers of Rome to be content with their wages (Luke 3:14). Paul claims, *I have learned how to get along happily whether I have much or little. I know how to live on almost nothing or with everything. I have learned the secret of contentment in every situation* (Philippians 4:11, 12, Living Bible).

All of the Bible passages are predicated on the truth that our source of all things is our heavenly Father. He is perfectly capable of taking care of our tomorrows just as He has met our needs today and in the past. Anchored in Him we are deeply secure and do not need the trappings of success as a security blanket.

Happily, Betty worked through her problem and now seeks her fulfillment of security from God. This has taken pressure off her relationship with her family and she and her husband have a whole new love affair going. He feels more adequate as a husband and she is fulfilled as a wife. They have learned that marriage is really a triangle. God is the top point while the husband and the wife are the bottom points. The closer they get to God the closer they get to each other.

The proverbist noted long ago *He that is greedy of gain troubleth his own house* (Proverbs 15:27). When we learn to seek emotional fulfillment from God, rather than man, we have a lesser need for possessions, and the resources we have go further.

Obeying God Signs the Check

Every person has an account in Heaven that can be tapped for earthly needs as well as future rewards in eternity. But not every person has access to that account. Only those who know and obey God have the resource of Heaven at their disposal. God clearly says, *Listen now! The Lord isn't too weak to save you. And He isn't getting deaf! He can hear you when you call! But the trouble is that your sins have cut you off from God. Because of sin he has turned his face away from you and will not listen anymore* (Isaiah 59:1, 2, Living Bible). Thus we see that obedience to God signs the check on the bank of Heaven. Without that signature we cannot increase our prosperity.

Just as disobedience cancels the blessings of God, so genuine obedience opens the treasure house. For example, one of the surprises involves the very pressing "time" problem. Note God's amazing promise to you, *My son, forget not my law; but let thine heart keep my commandments: For length of days, and long life, and peace, shall they add to thee* (Proverbs 3:1, 2). Imagine those three amazing gifts to you from God's treasurer: First, you will have more hours to your day; then, you will live longer on this earth, and finally, you will not be nearly as uptight as you have been.

Here is how it works. The first promise of more hours to your day merely means that God will help us get more done in less time. "Reverence for God adds hours to your day" is how one translation of the Scripture reads. Martin Luther said his life was so busy he simply could not afford to miss his devotional time with the Lord each morning. He found that when he skipped this, his day was lost in distractions. I have discovered the same thing. Our hours stretch when we give reverence to God.

Then, God promises a longer life to those who are obedient. This really makes sense. The true follower of Jesus will not be plagued with so many of the emotion-causing diseases that sap the world's strength. A rightness with God is reflected in better health as well as better wealth.

Finally, the proverbist notes the hours of the obedient believer are filled with peace, not turmoil. It is the way of the transgressor that is hard, not the way of the believer. The Christian doesn't have to worry about his lies or his sins catching up with him. He doesn't need to be concerned about bad gambling debts or about his mistress calling his wife. It is much more peaceful being a Christian than an unbeliever.

There is no question that obeying God brings great blessings. The Bible says, *Then shalt thou prosper, if you takest heed to fulfil the statutes and judgments which the Lord charged Moses with concerning Israel* (I Chronicles 22:13). It has been said so often it is almost a cliché, but we cannot avoid its truth. We are better off when we obey God.

Caring for the Needy

Most of the time the majority of us are on the borrowing end of a contract. But the Bible tells us how all of us can be on the lending end and at the same time reap windfall profits.

The proverbist advises, *When you help the poor you are lending to the Lord — and he pays wonderful interest on your loan*

(Proverbs 19:17, Living Bible). Then again, *If you give to the poor, your needs will be supplied! But a curse upon those who close their eyes to poverty* (Proverbs 28:27, Living Bible).

Lest this concept be thought a preacher's ploy to get more money for his church, talk with anyone who has tried it and you will find it works. In our church, for example, one man who owned a new business read this Scripture and began making missions a part of his sacrificial giving. God has blessed him so abundantly that now he cannot get enough employees to keep up with the expanding firm.

Volumes could and should be written of how those who have learned to give to the needy have been more blessed than ever before. It is true that God will remain a debtor to no man. He will abundantly bless, since he always pays His debts. Therefore, if you want more dollars, and you want the dollars you now have to go further, learn to give to missions sacrificially. The Bible is either true or false. If it is true, then here is one of the great clues to prosperity.

Millions of people in the world have starved to death, and we have all been shocked by news of earthquakes, and the tragedies of typhoons and war. What next? How can we feel so secure just because catastrophe has not yet struck us? How can we sit by and do nothing for disaster victims?

Amos was a rough farmer whom God pulled out of the pasture and sent into Bethel to needle King Jeroboam's violent, immoral society. Amos simply couldn't understand people who *trample the poor in the dust and kick aside the meek* (Amos 2:7, Living Bible). *Seek the Lord and live or else he will sweep like fire* (Amos 5:6, Living Bible).

Because of his fearless preaching, the life of Amos was exposed to constant danger. He earned the reputation of "God's angry man" because he hotly condemned the sins of Israel. Ironically, the Jews of a later generation considered him their greatest prophet, next to Isaiah. *Prepare to meet thy God* he declared, (Amos 4:12) and the wicked prophets of Bethel hated him. In fact Amaziah, leader of the Bethel prophets, tried to discredit his work and plotted his death. Tragedy came to Amaziah's home as a result of this diabolical scheme.

Amos saw three basic evils in Israel: prosperity had driven the people to wanton living; the poor people were being abused; and true worship was being replaced by Canaanite religions that emphasize irresponsibility. Amos called the people back to the worship of the one true God by reminding them that God is a Person, all-powerful, ever-present, all-knowing, ever-merciful, and alway righteous. He warned them that their continued sin would bring disaster. Within fifty years all of his prophecies had come true.

Four urgent lessons clearly come to us from the prophecies of Amos:

- The foundation for society rests on justice between men.
- Privilege implies responsibility.
- Failure to accept one's responsibility brings judgment.
- Nations and individuals must live up to all the light they have received.

If we live by these four great truths the face of our world will change.

God Invests in Givers

Prominent preacher Tommy Barnett says, "God invests in the stock market." What he means is that God also goes with a winner. The church that is doing great things for the Kingdom is the one that is growing and has the resources to do even more. This is a great Kingdom principle. The Bible says, *The liberal soul shall be made fat: and he that watereth shall be watered also himself* (Proverbs 11:25).

Earlier we noted that God's world operates on the principle of sowing and reaping, seedtime and harvest. Paul picks up on this point and says, *But remember this — if you give little, you will get little. A farmer who plants just a few seeds will get only a small crop, but if he plants much, he will reap much* (II Corinthians 9:6, Living Bible).

One of the first stories I heard my preacher dad tell was about the parson who took his boy to church. Before the service he showed the lad a new offering box he had put in the lobby and explained this was where the people gave their offering. To emphasize the point the father placed a shiny fifty cent piece in the box. After the service when the crowd had gone home the preacher went with his boy to open the offering box. To his dismay he found only the one coin there. The boy looked up at his father and said, "Well dad, if you would have put more in, you would have gotten more out."

Jesus talks about the same principle, *Try to show as much compassion as your Father does. Never criticize or condemn — or it will all come back on you. . . . For if you give, you will get! Your gift will return to you in full and overflowing measure, pressed down, shaken together to make room for more, and running over. Whatever measure you use to give — large or small — will be used to measure what is given back to you* (Luke 6:36-38, Living Bible). We get as we give.

Pay Our Tithes

In a later chapter we will deal more with tithing, but in the meantime it is important to understand how paying our tithes increases our income to stretch our dollars. The best place to check this is in The Book. The Bible says, *Will a man rob God? Surely not! And yet you have robbed me.*

"'What do you mean? When did we ever rob you?'

"You have robbed me of the tithes and offerings due to me. And so the awesome curse of God is cursing you, for your whole nation has been robbing me. Bring all the tithes into the storehouse so that there will be food enough in my Temple; if you do, I will open up the windows of heaven for you and pour out a blessing so great you won't have room enough to take it in!

"Try it! Let me prove it to you! Your crops will be large, for I will guard them from insects and plagues. Your grapes won't

shrivel away before they ripen," says the Lord of Hosts. "And all nations will call you blessed, for you will be a land sparkling with happiness. These are the promises of the Lord of Hosts" (Malachi, 3:8-12, Living Bible).

So there they are — five remarkable ways the Bible says you can increase your income and make your dollars go further.

- Look to God to meet physical, emotional and spiritual needs.
- Obey all the statutes of God.
- Care for the needy through practical love gifts, remembering that our giving is a loan to God.
- Be generous.
- Pay your tithes.

9

Profit Principles from the Prophets

William Northmore lost nearly a million dollars on the turn of a card. And that was two hundred years ago when his fortune was considerably larger than in today's inflationary market. Northmore of Okehampton, England, had inherited the fortune, and he soon degenerated into an inveterate gambler. Cards were what he loved most, but he would bet on anything, from the votes in parliament to which of several birds sitting on a wire would fly first.

After some success in gambling, Northmore met his downfall in the form of an ace of diamonds. With the turn of that one card his entire fortune was wiped out. This so shattered the young Englishman that he vowed never to gamble again. He stood by that promise and soon the townspeople of Okehampton saw the dramatic change. They voted him into Parliament in 1714 and returned him to that office in every election until his death. Athough he served well, still the great fortune he once had was never regained. His attempts to amass more money became a detour to poverty.

Gambling is always an attempt to take shortcuts to wealth. And whether the gamble is in Las Vegas or with chain letters, the end result is usually poverty. There are no shortcuts to real prosperity, although the Bible does give clear signposts along the way. It is those signposts to prosperity that we deal with here. God's

Word gives us several principles of profit from the prophets. The first of these is a strange one.

Don't Work for Money

A recent Harris survey reveals that North American men have great problems of dissatisfaction with their work. The poll reveals that 63 percent of males are not happy in their employment. This is a tragic commentary on our times and no wonder so many look forward to vacations and retirement. Perhaps the curse of sin does have much to do with our dissatisfaction, but I believe there is another major contributing factor: our quest for more money, shorter hours, and more benefits.

Many people make the tragic mistake of entering a profession or taking a position based on the monetary rewards. After all, our competitive society seems to demand that money is the sure status symbol of success. However, this is totally contrary to God's Word which says clearly, *Labour not to be rich* (Proverbs 23:4). Then the wise preacher adds, *The sleep of a labouring man is sweet, whether he eat little or much: but the abundance of the rich will not suffer him to sleep* (Ecclesiastes 5:12). I saw this example in the life of Bill.

Bill was a steel worker who had been with his company for many years. His salary had become tremendous and he was able to provide his family with a beautiful home, cars, boats, and all the other trappings of success. But Bill was desperately unhappy. After twenty years of marriage he began to physically abuse his wife. She couldn't understand what was happening. Although he was a Christian, he could not seem to control his outbursts of anger. Their home teetered on the brink of divorce with the children becoming more alienated from their parents every day. In this black state of affairs Bill and his wife came to me because they were ashamed to admit to their own pastor they were having these kinds of problems.

After a couple of sessions to determine the quality of their love, and to find out if they understood the Bible's premise that love is a responsibility — not a feeling — we discovered the problem was not their relationship at all. Rather, it was Bill's work. It was difficult for them to recognize the problem because Bill had been at his job for so long. He had received many raises and built up security, but he was desperately frustrated. He had repressed his unhappiness, feeling that everyone was destined to be unhappy in his work. However, when the middle age crisis came on, Bill started showing alarming symptoms. The Bible talks of this time of a person's life calling it, *the destruction that wasteth at noonday* (Psalm 91:6). Now the time of life, the growing family, and other anxieties had driven Bill to the breaking point.

When we confronted Bill with the problem, we asked, "If you could do anything you wanted with your life, what would it be?"

He immediately answered, "Oh, that's easy. I would start my own construction business and repair old houses."

"Then, why don't you do that?" I asked.

"I can't. We have financial obligations, I have so much seniority at work — then the construction business is so risky, especially now with our shaky economy," he hesitated.

But as we talked Bill began to see that it would be better to sweep the streets of his city for a living and be happy, than to make worlds of money and destroy his family. Destroying his family is exactly what he was doing and why the Bible says, *Better is a little with righteousness than great revenues without right* (Proverbs 16:8).

At that moment Bill made a decision and his wife agreed totally with it. I didn't see them for some time, then one day, much later, Bill's wife called me to say he had quit his old job. He had now attained his lifelong dream of his own business. And the best part was their home was happier than it had ever been. She just wanted to call and thank me.

One of the most important passages of the Bible that we often forget is, *Where there is no vision, the people perish* (Proverbs 29:18). I know this verse can be interpreted many ways, but, one of the ways I have found so true is that without a great cause in our lives, we dissipate into pettiness and misery. Money simply is not a big enough cause. I believe as long as the American public is hoodwinked by advertisers implying that money is the supreme thing — that products can make us happy — then we will continue to be miserable in our work and in our homes.

True prosperity cannot be measured by money. True prosperity is that inner rightness that only comes when our lives are in proper perspective with God and the world. That is why if we want to receive and enjoy God's best, the Bible tells us to get a greater goal than "filthy lucre."

Don't Expect a Free Lunch

One of the most difficult passages of Scripture is that which pertains to usury. Handling the Biblical concept of usury is especially hard for us in this society which runs on credit and has tax-deductible interest rates. Yet the Bible talks about this saying, *If your brother becomes poor, you are responsible to help him; invite him to live with you as a guest in your home. Fear your God and let your brother live with you; and don't charge him interest on the money you lend him. Remember — no interest; and give him what he needs at your cost: don't try to make a profit! For I, the Lord your God, brought you out of the land of Egypt to give you the land of Canaan, and to be your God* (Leviticus 25:35-38, Living Bible).

Usury was the sum paid for the use of money. The Israelites were forbidden to exact usury in their dealings with each other. However, with outsiders they were permitted to charge. *Don't demand interest on loans you make to a brother Israelite, whether it is in the form of money, food, or anything else. You may take interest from a foreigner, but not from an Israeli. For if you take interest from a brother, an Israeli, the Lord your God won't bless you when you arrive in the Promised Land* (Deuteronomy 23:19, 20, Living Bible).

Violation of this usury commandment was considered a grave offense. (Proverbs 28:8 and Psalm 15:5). After Israel returned from Babylon in captivity they neglected this commandment of God and were called to task harshly. Nehemiah heard that some of the rich Jews were profiteering off the less fortunate by charging interest on loans. He says, *I was very angry when I heard this; so after thinking about it I spoke out against these rich government officials.*

"What is this you are doing?" I demanded. "How dare you demand a mortgage as a condition for helping another Israelite?"

Then I called a public trial to deal with them. At the trial I shouted at them, "The rest of us are doing all we can to help our Jewish brothers who have returned from exile as slaves in distant lands, but you are forcing them right back into slavery again. How often must we redeem them?"

And they had nothing to say in their own defense.

Then I pressed further, "What you are doing is very evil," I exclaimed. "Should you not walk in the fear of our God? Don't we have enough enemies among the nations around us who are trying to destroy us?

"The rest of us are lending money and grain to our fellow-Jews without any interest. I beg you, gentlemen, stop this business of usury. Restore their fields, vineyards, oliveyards, and homes to them this very day and drop your claims against them" (Nehemiah 5:6-11, Living Bible). The Bible says they obeyed Nehemiah's suggestions and were blessed by their obedience.

Clearly there are two reasons for the prohibition of usury. The first and most important is that we must never take advantage of the unfortunate, creating more problems for them. The second reason is that God had given the rich their money and He intended they be as generous with it as He had been. By putting out their money to usury they were getting something for nothing. Rather than working for their money, they were letting their money work for them. They had an improper view of their possessions, and were so possessive they forgot that these things were given to them of God. Money was on loan to them from God so they could bless others. Their stinginess was making God very angry.

Without question, raw and ugly greed prompted these pampered rich to charge usury to their poor brothers. And is it not greed that makes gambling dens work? the race tracks flourish? and the palaces of passion possible? God hated usury because it made his people "grabbers" and "getters," rather than "givers" and "blessers."

All this brings up an important issue: If our brothers borrow from us, should we charge interest? I feel the general answer to this is, no, if he is in genuine need. However, if another merely wants to speculate with someone else's money, that is a different matter altogether.

Get Out of Debt

Some of the goals of communism are quite admirable. The idea that all men hold all things in common is a good one. However, it did not start with Karl Marx, but originated with God. God never intended for the very rich to take advantage of the very poor. In fact, His Word sets up an elaborate system of laws, that if followed, would result in an ideal community and government. Unfortunately man's greed has always got in the way.

Because we have an unbalanced world where the wealth is held in the hands of a few, it is a borrowing and lending society. In light of this fact it is important we learn what God's Word has to say, and then obey His commandments. The first general principle is that we should try to stay out of debt altogether. Paul noted, *Owe no man any thing, but to love one another* (Romans 13:8).

Knowing the ideal is to have no debts at all, still the Bible recognizes that there are times in our lives when circumstances demand indebtedness. Few of us have the ready cash to buy a home, or even a car. Therefore, the Bible also gives additional advice on our general attitude toward debt.

Responsibility toward our debts is shown in both Exodus and II Kings. Moses said the borrower of an animal who is injured or dies is responsible to pay back to the lender that which he borrowed. Also, when the axe head fell into the water while Elisha's students were building the Bible school, they knew they were expected to either retrieve it or replace it. This is why they were so concerned about the accident. So, we must be most responsible toward our debts. The Bible says, *The wicked borroweth and payeth not again: but the righteous sheweth mercy and giveth* (Psalm 37:21).

Again we see there is a warning about debt: *The rich ruleth over the poor, and the borrower is servant to the lender* (Proverbs 22:7).

While sitting in a financial seminar given by Dr. Al Holderness in Calcutta, India, God spoke to my own heart about the problem of owing money. I felt that He was telling me to get completely clear of all debts so I could better use my resources for missions. At that moment I made a pledge to do so and my life has been much less tense ever since. Although I would not presume to advise all persons to sell their homes and clear their debts, I do feel we need to be as free as possible so we can use our resources to reach this lost and lonely world for the Lord we love.

Perhaps a compromise would be in order. If indeed we cannot free ourselves of all debt, then the word of wisdom would be to obligate ourselves for only those things that appreciate as we keep them. We should eliminate "consumer credit" and debts for things that depreciate. I have found it is the charge accounts and the depreciating items in a debt budget that keep us handcuffed financially. Homes rise in value, as do some other properties.

But what about lending? Should we lend money to people if we have the resources to do so? Well, again the only word of wisdom we have is God's Word and that certainly is sufficient. Jesus said, *Give to him that asketh thee, and from him that would borrow of thee turn not thou away* (Matthew 5:42). Again, our Lord says, *But love ye your enemies, and do good, and lend, hoping for nothing again; and your reward shall be great, and ye shall be the children of the Highest: for He is kind unto the unthankful and to the evil* (Luke 6:35).

Moses said, *But if, when you arrive in the land the Lord will give you, there are any among you who are poor, you must not shut your heart or hand against them; you must lend them as much as they need. Beware! Don't refuse a loan because the year of debt cancellation is close at hand! If you refuse to make the loan and the needy man cries out to the Lord, it will be counted against you as sin. You must lend him what he needs, and don't moan about it either! For the Lord will prosper you in everything you do because of this! There will always be some among you who are poor; that is why this commandment is necessary. You must lend to them liberally* (Deuteronomy 15:7-11, Living Bible).

Often we quote the familiar Scripture about the righteous not begging bread. And it is a great assurance. However, we should read on, for it says, *I have been young and now I am old. And in all my years I have never seen the Lord forsake a man who loves him; nor have I seen the children of the godly go hungry. Instead, the godly are able to be generous with their gifts and loans to others, and their children are a blessing* (Psalm 37:25, 26, Living Bible). And again, *A good man sheweth favour, and lendeth; he will guide his affairs with discretion* (Psalm 112:5).

So the general rules for borrowing and lending are that:

- We should stay as free of debt as humanly possible.
- When we do acquire debts, we must be responsible to pay them.
- When God brings us to the Promised Land (prosperity) we have tremendous obligations to help those not as fortunate.
- We should give money and lend money to our brother who needs our help. My suggestion is that if he is a brother in the Lord, and the loan is for a legitimate need, no interest should be charged.

I think with these general ideas in mind we can move safely through financial waters.

Don't Cosign a Note

A great deal of emotional pressure can be brought on us to cosign notes for friends, family, and loved ones. However, we must keep in mind that the Bible discourages us from doing so. *Son, if you endorse a note for someone you hardly know, guaranteeing his debt, you are in serious trouble. You may have trapped yourself by your agreement. Quick! Get out of it if you possibly can! Swallow your pride; don't let embarrassment stand in the way. Go and beg to have your name erased. Don't put it off. Do it now. Don't rest until you do. If you can get out of this trap you have saved yourself like a deer that escapes from a hunter, or a bird from the net* (Proverbs 6:1-5, Living Bible).

If we are still in doubt about the wisdom of cosigning, we read on, *Be sure you know a person well before you vouch for his credit! Better refuse than suffer later* (Proverbs 11:15, Living Bible).

Then, *It is poor judgment to countersign another's note, to become responsible for his debt* (Proverbs 17:18, Living Bible).

Finally, there is a bitter warning, *Unless you have the extra cash on hand, don't countersign a note. Why risk everything you own? They'll even take your bed!* (Proverbs 22:26, 27, Living Bible).

I have seen much personal pain result because parents countersigned notes for their children, or friends for other friends. It is much better to loan or give a person money directly, than be surety for him. If we don't have the resources to give or loan, then that should be a warning to us that we should not countersign. I know that this commandment is hard to live by, especially in our society with so many "get rich quick" schemes, but the Bible is to be believed and obeyed if we want to prosper.

Dr. Smiley Blanton, longtime psychiatrist on East Coast, had a Bible on his desk in plain view for all patients to see. When one would ask him about it, he always replied, "If people would read and live what the Bible says all we psychiatrists would close our doors and go fishing." I tend to agree with him. If we lived the principles of God's Word we would be happier, healthier, and no doubt richer.

Not only does the Bible talk about personal wealth, but also, as you will see, gives good advice to the businessman.

10

How to Make Your Business Grow

"You're crazy, preacher," the arrogant young businessman told me. "If you think you can apply the principles of Jesus Christ to today's business world, you're insane." Tim went on to add, "They are vultures out there and they would eat you up if you tried. I'm sorry, but you just don't understand. Wake up and join the real world."

My friend was the president of a growing insurance firm and was making all kinds of money. He and his wife had invited my wife and me to dinner and before long I had turned the conversation to talking about Christ. His wife was visibly moved and even in the busy, exclusive restaurant, began to cry as we talked. That's when Tim shot his angry words at me.

I tried to persuade my friend he was wrong, but his mind was locked in gear and he would have nothing of my reasoning. He implied that a preacher might be alright at delivering a harmless homily on Sunday mornings to a few old ladies who perhaps were feebleminded anyway and had little to live for, but he had nothing to say to a vibrant and successful businessman who knew what it was all about and had proven he could make it on his own.

Somewhat embarrassed by his attack, Tim's wife changed the subject and we drifted into safer and less stormy waters. My heart was saddened as we left them that night. I felt his wife had really wanted to make a commitment to Christ, but the brashness of her husband had caused her to withdraw.

Two years passed before I heard about Tim again. Then, it was only through a newspaper story that carried the heartbreaking account of how he killed himself at the age of thirty-six. There were hints that something had gone wrong with his business and Tim knew of nowhere else to turn but into the barrel of a .38.

The Bible is right when it says, *He that trusteth in his own heart is a fool: but whoso walketh wisely, he shall be delivered* (Proverbs 28:26). Although it may take a little longer for the righteous man to arrive at the peak of financial success, it is still the only way to travel. That must have been what the psalmist meant when he said, *Only with thine eyes shalt thou behold and see the reward of the wicked* (Psalm 91:8). Or, it only appears on the surface that the evil prosper. Real prosperity cannot come to them and certainly would never stay if it did come. They might have money in the bank, but no peace in their hearts.

As we read God's Word we find He has much to say about business. We also discover, *Thus saith the Lord, thy Redeemer, the Holy One of Israel; I am the Lord thy God which teacheth thee to profit, which leadeth thee by the Way that thou shouldest go* (Isaiah 48:17). What better teacher could we have or want than our Creator who has instituted all laws of prosperity?

Understanding that He indeed wants us to prosper, let us sit at His feet and learn a few principles that will make our businesses grow. There are many in God's Word but here for the sake of brevity, we share only four.

Be Honest in All Your Dealings

Bilking customers out of pennies has now become a billion-dollar business. The *National Observer* has noted that short weighing on food, gasoline, home fuel oil, packaged hardware items, and pills costs the American public some six to twelve billion dollars per year. In an effort to curb this swindle, whether accidental or intentional, many states are spot-checking weights and measures.

Pennsylvania investigators discovered that 15.5 percent of all prepackaged foods checked were short weighted, with some stores shorting on 25 percent of the packages checked. A three-day Kansas investigation turned up evidence that 30 percent of all meat packaged in eleven stores were short weighted. In Arkansas, officials checked one-pound cans of vegetables to find none that contained sixteen ounces; and Tennessee officials found pre-packaged pork chops short weighted by up to a cost of thirty-one cents per package. Officials have tabulated forty-eight ways to cheat in weighing meat in front of customers, and many markets are apparently using some of them.

All of this reveals the avarice deep within the hearts of men, as well as a basic dishonesty in our striving for materialistic gain. This cheating on small things seems to be a tragic commentary on our society.

"Where does sin start?" seems to be a question many are asking. Is it evil to cheat for pennies, or does "right" have a price tag on it? Tragically, many feel the results of these smaller swindles, but hardly raise an eyebrow as they are perpetrated. Under-the-table deals and payoffs are often accepted in our society as we shrug our shoulders and let them go unnoticed.

Thoughtful people may ponder and debate where evil starts, but the Bible is very clear. Christ gave many parables about honesty and responsibility, declaring that man's avarice begins in the heart and does not have a price tag. It is just as dishonest to steal a penny as it is to steal a million dollars.

Jesus said it this way: *He that is faithful in that which is least is faithful also in much: and he that is unjust in the least is unjust also in much* (Luke 16:10).

Many of our nations' youth have become disenchanted with our moral values because they seem to be on a sliding scale. Situational ethics is really no ethics at all. Jesus drew the line between good and evil very clearly, and said boldly that we should be on one side or the other. Unlike earthly teachers, God does not grade on a curve.

Trying to excuse our small dishonesties, we often say, "At least I haven't murdered, committed adultery, or robbed a bank." Yet one does not have to break all the laws of the land to be considered a criminal. Similarly, one does not have to break every commandment to be a sinner. The Bible simply states, *For whosoever shall keep the whole law, and yet offend in one point, he is guilty of all* (James 2:10).

Four times in the Book of Proverbs it is noted, *A false balance is abomination to the Lord: but a just weight is his delight.* Obviously, honesty in the small things is important to our Creator. Sin is a seed that grows until one day it overwhelms us. If we erase the mark between good and evil to inch it further with each situation, before long we find our own avarice has moved us to forget the line completely. Jesus clearly states that the time to stop evil is at its conception.

Stories of Abraham Lincoln's honesty in walking miles to return a few pennies he overcharged, warm our hearts, for we admire honesty. However, this should be the norm, with the dishonest being the exception. But it seems today that when one steps out to be honest he is almost laughed out of the ball park.

If Christ cannot trust us with the little things, surely He cannot trust us with bigger things. This includes expense accounts, tax forms, and petty cash. Conversely, those who are honest and just in the little things are those God trusts with the great things in His kingdom — if we are faithful in a few things, He will make us ruler over many.

Thus we see that the first cardinal rule of business is honesty. Honesty may be old-fashioned and seemingly a slower way to get to our goals, but the Bible assures us that it is the only way.

Don't Take Advantage of Hardship

Our world is imperfect and life is so structured that storms do come. People will be wiped out by floods, tornadoes, and financial disasters. Job sadly observed *Man that is born of a woman is of a few days, and full of trouble* (Job 14:1).

The Bible is very clear when it says we are not to take advantage of bad times to make high profits. Right now there is deep hostility toward the Arabs and the giant oil companies because many feel, rightly or wrongly, that they are taking advantage of the energy crisis to build their financial empires. A whole bureaucracy has been set up in Washington to deal with price gouging.

But the Bible warns, *Dishonest gain will never last, so why take the risk? Because the wicked are unfair, their violence boomerangs and destroys them* (Proverbs 21:6, 7, Living Bible). Note the words that precede these two verses, *Steady plodding brings prosperity; hasty speculation brings poverty* (Proverbs 21:5, Living Bible).

It is hard for us to see how giant corporations or power blocks can be wiped out as these verses suggest, but perhaps we should remember Hitler. Standing proud in his power, pomp, and glory, he presented an invincible image to the frightened world. But, as we all know, Hitler did not succeed in breaking God's law; he only broke himself on it.

The Bible becomes even more specific about taking advantage of bad times. Amos lashes out against the businessmen of his day, *You trample the poor and steal their smallest crumb by all your taxes, fines, and usury; therefore you will never live in the beautiful stone houses you are building, nor drink the wine from the lush vineyards you are planting* (Amos 5:11, Living Bible).

John the Baptist told the collectors of taxes, *Make sure you collect no more taxes than the Roman government requires you to* (Luke 3:13, Living Bible).

Perhaps the strongest Bible statement about taking advantage of the misfortunes of others is simply, *He who gains by oppressing the poor or by bribing the rich shall end in poverty . . . Don't rob the poor and sick! For the Lord is their defender. If you injure them he will punish you* (Proverbs 22:16, 22, 23, Living Bible).

Jeremiah became upset with those who oppressed the poor and he rose in eloquent anger, *Like a bird that fills her nest with young she has not hatched and which will soon desert her and fly away, so is the man who gets his wealth by unjust means. Sooner or later he will lose his riches and at the end of his life become a poor old fool* (Jeremiah 17:11, Living Bible).

Not only is there a warning, but also there is promise. Isaiah said to the businessmen of Israel, *Feed the hungry! Help those in trouble! Then your light will shine out from the darkness, and the darkness around you shall be as bright as day. And the Lord will guide you continually, and satisfy you with all good things, and keep you healthy too; and you will be like a well-watered garden, like an ever-flowing spring* (Isaiah 58:10,11, Living Bible).

Interestingly enough, Isaiah talks about honoring the Lord's day in this same passage. It would be well to note what he says: *If you keep the Sabbath holy, not having your own fun and business that day, but enjoying the Sabbath and speaking of it with delight as the Lord's holy day, and honoring the Lord in what you do, not following your own desires and pleasure, nor talking idly — then the Lord will be your delight, and I will see to it that you ride high, and get your full share of the blessings I promised to Jacob, your father. The Lord has spoken* (Isaiah 58:13, 14, Living Bible).

Before we leave this important point of not taking advantage of those in difficulty, we need to remember that very seldom does the Bible record Jesus being angry. However, there were a couple of times. One, of course, was when He cleansed the temple of the people who had turned God's house into a marketplace and blocked access to the House of Prayer. Then, the second occasion was when Jesus wanted to heal a man with a withered hand on the Sabbath. Knowing He would be called into question for His action, Jesus asked the Pharisees if it were good to do good or evil on the Sabbath day. The Pharisees, knowing they could not answer the question and still trap Jesus for Sabbath violation, refused to answer. At that moment Jesus burned with anger because they totally ignored the need of the man standing before them. Here is what Mark records: *Looking around at them angrily, for he was deeply disturbed by their indifference to human need, he said to the man, "Reach out your hand." He did, and instantly his hand was healed* (Mark 3:5, Living Bible).

It is very easy to take advantage of the weak and needy. When a man needs a loan, it is possible to extort more from him than is fair. When his children are hungry because of a natural calamity, great fortunes can be made. But, God forbid that we ever do that. The Bible says, *Woe to unjust judges and to those who issue unfair laws, says the Lord, so that there is no justice for the poor, the widows and the orphans. Yes, it is true that they even rob the widows and fatherless children.*

Oh, what will you do, Isaiah asks of God, *when I visit you in that day when I send desolation upon you from a distant land? To whom will you turn then for your help? Where will your treasures be safe? I will not help you; you will stumble along as prisoners or lie among the slain. And even then my anger will not be satisfied, but my fist will still be poised to strike you* (Isaiah 10:1-4, Living Bible).

Clearly, fairness is the guiding principle here. And that fairness is also to be observed when dealing with personnel problems.

Deal Fairly with Employees

"I was carried on a silver platter and then dumped into the garbage can." These were the bitter words of former child actor Bobby Driscoll just before his tragic death at the age of thirty-one. He was found March 30, 1968, lying dead on a cot inside an abandoned tenement building, by children exploring the old house. Beside his body were religious pamphlets and two empty beer bottles. No one recognized the former child star; in fact, for two years his body was buried in a pauper's grave in New York's City Cemetery. Identity was finally traced through fingerprints, and his mother then notified of her only child's death.

Cause of death was "occlusive coronary arteriosclerosis," or hardening of the arteries, a condition common in longtime users of heroin. By his own admission Bobby had been a heavy user of hard drugs for years. Each time he had tried to make a comeback, life seemed to fall in on him. Known best for his part in the popular Walt Disney movie, "Song of the South," Bobby shot to fame overnight. But by 1954 he was no longer needed as a child actor and was turned out. He was totally frustrated and angry because of how he had been used and then dumped.

Although "Song of the South" has been reissued and is enjoying great success again, there will be no reruns for the cherub-faced Bobby. His story is a tragic testimony to a popular game in our society: that of using, manipulating, maneuvering lives to selfish advantage. Many people merchandise men and women as if they were products, caring nothing for the delicate souls inside the beautiful exteriors. Lives such as those of Marilyn Monroe and Bobby Driscoll point to the horror of such atrocities.

God's Word gives strong warning against such merchandising.

And their mouth speaketh great swelling words, having men's persons in admiration because of advantage (Jude 16).

There are many who flatter for selfish advantage, who use people, regardless of the hurt they cause or grief they bring. Such crass disregard does not go unnoticed by God. Jesus talked frankly about such a problem and warned: *But whoso shall offend one of these little ones which believe in me, it were better for him that a millstone were hanged about his neck, and that he were drowned in the depth of the sea. Woe unto the world because of offences! for it must needs be that offences come; but woe to that man by whom the offence cometh!* (Matthew 18:6, 7).

Understanding that God demands we be fair with our employees, we move on to learn specific commandments regarding wages, attitudes, and management. It is perhaps somewhat surprising to some to learn that long before there were unions, God demanded that the godly businessman be fair with his employees, especially when it comes to money. The Bible tells the employer to pay promptly, pay a living wage, and not to withhold more than is required.

Moses deals frankly and openly with businessmen who take advantage of their employees. Note what he says about paying wages promptly: *Never oppress a poor hired man, whether a fellow Israelite or a foreigner living in your town. Pay him his wage each day before sunset, for since he is poor he needs it right away; otherwise he may cry out to the Lord against you and it would be counted as a sin against you* (Deuteronomy 24:14, 15, Living Bible).

Add to this, *You shall not rob nor oppress anyone, and you shall pay your hired workers promptly. If something is due them, don't even keep it overnight* (Leviticus 19:13, Living Bible). In other words God wants us to pay on time and pay fairly: to withhold is to steal, since the money is no longer ours when the work is complete.

What about those employers who hire workers then refuse to pay them at all? Note the bitterness of Jeremiah's curse when he says, *And woe to you, King Jehoiakim, for you are building your great palace with forced labour. By not paying wages you are building injustice into its walls and oppression into its doorframes and ceilings. You say, "I will build a magnificent palace with huge rooms and many windows, paneled throughout with fragrant cedar and painted a lovely red." But a beautiful palace does not make a great king! Why did your father Josiah reign so long? Because he was just and fair in his dealings. That is why God blessed him. He saw to it that justice and help were given the poor and the needy and all went well for him. This is how a man lives close to God. But you! You are full of selfish greed and all dishonesty! You murder the innocent, oppress the poor and reign with ruthlessness* (Jeremiah 22:13-17, Living Bible).

In verse 19, Jeremiah then goes on to declare that because of the wicked king's attitude God would bury him like a dead donkey — he would be dragged out of Jerusalem and thrown on a garbage dump.

And that is exactly what happened.

The Bible also warns about fraudulent withholding of wages. James sharply rebukes the profiteers of his day by quoting God, *Look here, you rich men, now is the time to cry and groan with anguished grief because of all the terrible troubles ahead of you. Your wealth is even now rotting away, and your fine clothes are becoming mere moth-eaten rags. The value of your gold and silver is dropping fast, yet it will stand as evidence against you, and eat your flesh like fire. That is what you have stored up for yourselves, to receive on that coming day of judgment. For listen! Hear the cries of the field workers whom you have cheated of their pay. Their cries have reached the ears of the Lord of hosts* (James 5:1-4, Living Bible).

Finally, still in the area of finance, the prophet Malachi warns employers about failure to pay a living wage: *And I will come near to you to judgment; and I will be a swift witness against the sorcerers, and against the adulterers, and against false swearers, and against those that oppress the hireling in his wages, the widow, and the fatherless, and that turn aside the stranger from his right, and fear not me, saith the Lord of hosts* (Malachi 3:5).

There are many other admonitions in our relationships with our employees that cover both attitude and judgment. In Job's final defense of his righteousness he knew God carefully watched how he treated his employees. Therefore he says, *If I have been unfair to my servants, how could I face God? . . . For God made me, and my servant too. He created us both.*

If I have hurt the poor, Job continues, *or caused the widows to weep, or refused food to the hungry orphans — (but we have always cared for orphans in our home, treating them as our own children) — or if I have seen anyone freezing and not given him clothing, or fleece from my sheep to keep him warm, or if I have taken advantage of an orphan because I thought I could get away with it — if I have done any of these things, then let my arm be torn from its socket! Let my shoulder be wrenched out of place! Rather that than face the judgment sent by God; that I dread more than anything else. For if the majesty of God opposes me, what hope is there?* (Job 31:13-23).

Paul the apostle would write to two churches telling them to be careful in their dealings with their employees. He says to the people of Ephesus, *And you slave owners must treat your slaves right, just as I have told them to treat you. Don't keep threatening them; remember, you yourselves are slaves to Christ; you have the same Master they do, and he has no favorites* (Ephesians 6:9, Living Bible).

Then to the businessmen of Colosse he admonishes, *You slave owners must be just and fair to all your slaves. Always remember that you, too, have a Master in heaven who is closely watching you* (Colossians 4:1, Living Bible). Certainly if we want our businesses to grow we must be fair with the employees God has given us.

There is one final admonition that perhaps is personal, but I believe it important. That is we are to hire and be in partnership only with believers. Note what Paul says to the church at Corinth: *Don't be teamed with those who do not love the Lord, for what do the people of God have in common with the people of sin?* (II Corinthians 6:14, Living Bible).

In the King James version the word picture Paul uses is that of a yoke. We must remember that a yoke is a working arrangement. Therefore, I feel it wise to hire and form business partnerships only with those who are believers, although I know this statement could bring charges of discrimination. When I have advocated this, many have said to me that as a preacher I cannot possibly understand the pressures of trying to find good and qualified employees, and that my suggestion is illegal. Perhaps they are right and I am wrong. But for a business that is dedicated to God's work, I believe the idea is a good one.

When I have talked at length with businessmen about this concept they have argued, sometimes at length, that my position is too idealistic. And perhaps it is. However, why is it that we can trust God to provide finances for ourselves and our businesses, but we cannot trust him to provide Christian employees? As a minister of Jesus Christ, I see no difference in hiring an unbeliever in a Christian business as I do in hiring an unbeliever as an important staff member of a church. After all, what makes the church any more of a ministry than a Christian business?

I know these principles are touchy and subject at times to personal interpretation. However, I think we should consider them and ask our Lord to be in full charge of our businesses. He is perfectly capable of providing the financial resources — and the employees — we need. We should make our workers a matter of deep spiritual concern and prayer.

Take Care of Our Businesses

Rock star Elvis Presley insisted that his employees wear a button on their coats with the letters, TCB. When asked about the meaning of this cryptic message he simply would reply, "It means Take Care of the Business." He knew that unless watched diligently the business would die or dissipate into losses. The Bible notes the same thing. Paul says, *Not slothful in business; fervent in spirit; serving the Lord* (Romans 12:11). The proverbist writes, *He becometh poor that dealeth with a slack hand: but the hand of the diligent maketh rich* (Proverbs 10:4). Again, *The soul of the sluggard desireth, and hath nothing: but the soul of the diligent shall be made fat* (Proverbs 13:4). And once again, *Seest thou a man diligent in his business? he shall stand before kings; he shall not stand before men* (Proverbs 22:29).

With the present energy crisis, many employers are learning again the wisdom of the Bible's advice. We are relearning that businesses fail because they lose in small ways. These small things drain us because we fail to plug up the holes through lack of attention.

In a report on the energy crisis, *Time* magazine pointed out one simple area in which diligence pays. It said:

> While much of the public continues to behave as if there were a Constitutional mandate to expend energy — the nation will burn some four percent more oil this year (1979) than in 1978 — corporate consumers are discovering that saving fuel is a simple way to cut costs and boost profits. Ever since the 1973 oil embargo, companies have been turning off lights, lowering thermostats, redesigning buildings, and driving the conservation message home to employees.
>
> Some measures are as sophisticated as the elaborate computer system Burlington Industries installed to regulate electrical use in 20 plants. Others are as simple as the discovery by General Motors that it could save $1576 a year by removing fluorescent bulbs in its shop-floor vending machines.
>
> As a result, according to Department of Energy officials, the savings to business are estimated at nearly $3 billion since 1974.

So we learn that four of the Bible's principles of making your business grow are,

- Be honest in your dealings.
- Don't take advantage of hardship.
- Deal fairly with your employees.
- Be diligent in your business.

Later we will learn that God has some strong things to say to all of us who work for businesses and how we are to function as Christian workers.

11

Giving Is Not the Answer

In our complex world we are always looking for simple answers — but usually things are not as clear-cut as we would like. The following classic story of the evasive criminal underlines this point.

The accused stood before the judge and managed to evade every direct question asked of him. Finally, his honor exploded in anger and rapped the gavel loudly shouting, "Answer the questions, yes or no!"

"But your honor," the offender offered, "There are some questions to which you just can't answer yes or no."

Seething with anger the judge challenged, "That just isn't true. Show me one question you can't answer with a simple yes or no."

"Have you stopped beating your wife?" the wiley criminal asked the embarrassed judge.

Perhaps one of the great problems we have in our age is that we try to simplify everything to the point that truth is sometimes distorted. Maybe that is what has happened with some of our "prosperity preachers." Without doubt many of them are good men who love their Lord, but what we often hear said is a distortion of the "whole truth." And too often people act on what they *think* truth is, rather than what truth is. This is especially so when it comes to speakers encouraging believers to give to their ministries.

One Scripture used by many (so much it has become almost a cliché) is, *Give, and it shall be given unto you; good measure, pressed down, and shaken together, and running over, shall men give into your bosom. For with the same measure that ye mete withal it shall be measured to you again* (Luke 6:38). There is no question about the statement being true. Christ would never have said it if it were not. And earlier in this book we too used the same Scripture. But we must remember that it must be obeyed in light of *all* the teachings of our Lord, not just as an isolated text standing alone in naked splendor.

When we study "texts" rather than the Bible, we can get a distorted view of what God's Word says. That is why a person who reads the Bible only in times of crisis can totally misunderstand the meaning of God's Word. There must be a continual reading or we will isolate Scriptures to reinforce our own beliefs. This is how cults spring up with their own particular interpretation of their pet texts. It would be well to remember the angel admonished the apostles when he let them out of prison, *Go, stand and speak in the temple to the people all the words of this life* (Acts 5:20). Note, the angel said, "all the words." Add to this Paul's defense before the Ephesian elders, *For I have not shunned to declare unto you all the counsel of God* (Acts 20:27).

It was this tendency to isolate texts that prompted Henry Drummond to comment, "To see some small soul pirouetting throughout life on a single text and judging all the world because it cannot find a partner, is not a Christian sight." We must keep in mind that one of the most effective ministries of the Holy Spirit is *comparing spiritual things with spiritual* (I Corinthians 2:13).

So in understanding this beautiful promise of our Lord concerning giving and receiving, let us see what else the Bible has to say.

Jesus Himself said that giving alone is not the answer. "How" we give is just as important as "what" we give. If our giving brings the blessings our Lord promises us, then we must learn the principles of sowing according to His Word. Just as a farmer must place a seed in the ground, water and tend that seed according to the laws of harvest before a crop grows, so, we cannot sow whatever we wish if we want to reap prosperity. Rather, we must give according to the prescription of our heavenly Father. That is why we emphatically say that giving alone is not the answer.

There are at least six instructions to be considered from God's Word about how to give. They are: according to ability; without fanfare; liberally; simply; regularly; and cheerfully. If we plant as God tells us to, then the magnificent promise of Jesus will indeed come true.

Give According to Ability

God has never asked us for what we cannot give. From the first foundational laws of giving we learn, *Every man shall give as he is able, according to the blessing of the Lord thy God which he hath given thee* (Deuteronomy 16:17).

When Moses talked of sacrifices he said, *And he shall offer one of the turtledoves, or of the young pigeons, such as he can get* (Leviticus 14:30).

Unlike some religions that demand the resources of a lifetime's work, God set up a percentage plan that was equitable for all men. In rebuilding the temple Ezra notes: *They gave after their ability unto the treasure of the work* (Ezra 2:69). Any ministry of religion that demands more than what God's Word allows, should be looked upon with deep suspicion.

About the New Testament pattern of giving, the Bible says, *Then the disciples, every man according to his ability, determined to send relief unto the brethren which dwelt in Judaea* (Acts 11:29).

Paul adds, *If you are really eager to give, then it isn't important how much you have to give. God wants you to give what you have, not what you haven't.* Then, he goes on: *Of course I don't mean that those who receive your gifts should have an easy time of it at your expense, but you should divide with them. Right now you have plenty and can help them; then at some other time they can share with you when you need it. In this way each will have as much as he needs. Do you remember what the Scriptures say about this? "He that gathered much had nothing left over, and he that gathered little had enough."* (II Corinthians 8:12-15, Living Bible).

Not long ago a distraught couple came into my office for

counseling. In frustration they spilled out their story. They told me they had been listening to a number of preachers who reminded them (correctly) that God will be a debtor to no man. They had been encouraged to give sacrificially and they would receive abundantly. They had done so even up to 30 percent of their income. However, the laws of God had not worked for them. Rather than prospering they were getting deeper in debt.

"What is wrong?" they asked. "Why doesn't giving work for us?"

In answer to their sincere questions I suggested they cut back their giving to the amount God told them to contribute in His Word. (In the next chapter we will deal with how much, and where, God wants us to invest our giving dollars.) I shared with them the principles of financial responsibility and talked about how they were spending their remaining 70 percent. Thankfully, this beautiful couple responded to the counseling and today they once again are on strong financial ground. God thoroughly understands that we have certain earthly needs that must be satisfied. Our needs will be met if we respond obediently to His Word. He tells us we are to give according to ability. God does not wish to see any of His children bear more of the load than someone else.

This principle can and will be argued by those who disagree with my premise. And that is their privilege. However, as a pastor I have dealt with the misunderstandings of some very good people who have been misled. I know greed has prompted some to "give to get," but aside from these, others who really want to help the Kingdom have gotten themselves financially strapped. I suppose that is why both Jeremiah and Ezekiel call irresponsible spiritual leaders to task. Note how sharp the rebuke is to Israel's leaders who had misled the people. You can read about it in both Ezekiel 34 and Jeremiah 23.

Give Without Fanfare

Jesus was most adamant about giving without fanfare. He says, *Take care! Don't do your good deeds publicly, to be admired, for then you will lose the reward from your Father in heaven. When you give a gift to a beggar, don't shout about it as the hypocrites do — blowing trumpets in the synagogues and streets to call attention to their acts of charity! I tell you in all earnestness, they have received all the reward they will ever get. But when you do a kindness to someone, do it secretly — don't tell your left hand what your right hand is doing. And your Father who knows all secrets will reward you* (Matthew 6:1-4, Living Bible).

As we will learn later giving is a part of worship, and worship really is a very private matter. The soul lies next to the heart of God and our acts of worship are sacred and secret between Him and us alone. Just as the intimate acts of marriage are reserved for the couple and will suffer tremendous harm if shared with others, so talk about giving loses its reward.

Johnny Cash is a classic and positive example. The world knows this famous country singer has turned his heart to the Lord, but I learned firsthand about the depth of his commitment when we were building a chapel at Tucker Prison. While chaplain there I had the responsibility of arranging for the social life of the inmates as well as their spiritual welfare. In that role I met and asked the Country King to come to the prison and present a program for us. He agreed to do so, saying that I was not to let the press or public know the financial arrangements. He did not want his "gift" known to others.

Now that the years have passed, I think it would be okay with Mr. Cash if I told what happened. Johnny brought his whole troupe, about thirty people, at his own expense. He refused to accept a dime for the program and gave the inmates one of the finest afternoons of entertainment they had ever received. But there was more than that.

Johnny learned we were building a chapel for our men and that I had been traveling throughout the state raising money for it. There were no state funds available so I had to go to various church people. Never in the history of this prison had the men had their own place of worship, nor had there ever been a full-time chaplain. When Johnny learned these things, he called me over privately. He wrote out a $5,000 check for the chapel, warning me that I was not to let anyone know of that gift. I suppose that even today his troupe is totally unaware of it. Here was a man who simply loved his Lord and wanted to do something for the Kingdom.

My esteem for Johnny Cash was greatly enhanced that day. Regardless of whether a person enjoys country music, there is no question that this great Christian lives the commands of Christ to give in simplicity. I have never doubted as to why he has been so tremendously blessed. The Father, who saw in secret, rewarded Johnny Cash openly.

Make It Simple

Giving to God is not really complicated. In fact, the Bible says, *he that giveth, let him do it with simplicity* (Romans 12:8).

There are so many needs in our world that most of us have our mailboxes stuffed with appeals from various religious organizations asking us to contribute to this ministry or that. Sometimes it becomes a complicated decision for us to determine where we should give our resources. Should we send them to this preacher or that one? It is a legitimate question that demands an answer.

Not long ago a group of ministers met together to establish guidelines for their people in giving to various ministries. They used questions like, "Are they preaching the full Gospel?" and "How much of their money is actually given to the work and how much goes to support the evangelist?" They even suggested not supporting an evangelist unless he made a full disclosure of his finances. Well, all these suggestions are good, and perhaps should be considered, but frankly, I feel there is a much simpler answer.

When two people live together through the years of marriage one can almost anticipate the thoughts of the other. And the closer they walk to each other, the softer they need to speak to be heard. Therein is the answer. The closer we walk to our Lord and the longer we love Him, the easier the decision becomes as to where to channel our resources. I have found God speaks to my heart through gentle impressions. There are no flashing lights or "signs in the sky." Rather, when I receive an appeal, if I am drawn toward the need, I give. If not, I ignore it. There have been times when I have thrown an appeal away, only to go back to the wastebasket, draw it out, and send a check. The gentle but persistent voice of my Lord would not let me go.

Thus, the answer of where to give (after tithing) is really rather simple. If we walk closely with our Lord, and if He has given us a love and concern for a certain minister or ministry, then these gentle impulses are probably His way of speaking to us. We have to remember that God didn't speak to Elijah through the fire, earthquake, or wind; but through a still small voice. Don't be afraid to follow your heart. Our Lord will lead you and certainly lift the burden from your soul if the ministry to which you contribute no longer has His blessings.

Give Regularly

Over the past year the government of the United States has been putting pressure on television ministers and evangelists because of emotional appeals over the airwaves. Of course, there is danger on both sides of this river bank. On the one hand it is not right for continued emotional appeals that drain needed resources from people who do not have them to give. But there is also a danger of choking off freedom of religion in our country. We need to pray for wisdom that this great missionary country of ours will not be knocked to its knees because some politician wants to kill a fly with a sledgehammer.

Perhaps one of the best ways we can solve the problem is to learn to obey God's Words in responding more to regular giving than to emotional appeals. Paul tells us, *Upon the first day of the week let every one of you lay by him in store, as God hath prospered him, that there be no gatherings when I come* (I Corinthians 16:2).

Paul did not want to be known as a fund raiser; he wanted to spend his time ministering to the needs of people. Therefore, if the people learned to give regularly, rather than on the basis of an emotional appeal, the church of the Lord Jesus Christ would march forward, not deterred by lack of funds. It is an excellent premise.

I have seen this principle work and bring great blessings to God's people.

In my early ministry I was called to a church that had got into deep financial trouble through severe problems with the pastor and people. When I arrived the church was seven months behind on its mortgage payment, and two weeks later we were served foreclosure notices. Believing that God will honor His word I told the board that there were to be no great emotional pleas. Rather, the people would be informed of the needs of the church during regular offering times, and if God could not provide for these needs then the church building would just have to go.

The miracle is that we did not lose the church. Rather, the church prospered abundantly, and within one year we had not only caught up with the mortgage payments, but had also wiped out nearly $30,000 worth of past due accounts. The reason for this miracle was not the power or personality of the preacher, but because God's people began to obey God and lay aside every week what God had told them to give.

God always honors His Word. That is why Isaiah notes, *As the rain and snow come down from heaven and stay upon the ground to water the earth, and cause the grain to grow and to produce seed for the farmer and bread for the hungry, so also is my Word. I send it out and it always produces fruit. It shall accomplish all I want it to, and prosper everywhere I send it. You will live in joy and peace. The mountains and hills, the trees of the field — all the world around you — will rejoice. Where once were thorns, fir trees will grow; where briars grew, the myrtle trees will sprout up* (Isaiah 55:10-13), Living Bible).

Give Freely

John Chapman had received much and he wanted to give much. He decided to leave his home in Springfield, Massachusetts and travel the country planting apple trees. He loved apples and that love, combined with his religious convictions, drove him on. For forty-five years Johnny walked through the eastern United States and covered more than 100,000 square miles. He retraced his steps over and over again to cultivate and to prune the trees he planted.

Along the way, Johnny drew attention with his eccentric garb — a coffee sack for a shirt and a tin pot for a hat. In his hat he would cook his meals. He distributed Bibles as well, even though many would disagree with his unusual approach to understanding Scriptures. He fondly began to be known throughout the country as "Johnny Appleseed," a name that has stuck through the years.

Johnny Appleseed was a folk hero in his own day, and his legend seems to have grown with the passage of time. The orchards that now dot many parts of the United States are a memorial to his love for the land, his apples, his fellowman, and his God.

Jesus lets us know that a great responsibility comes with the blessings He gives us. Therefore, if our offerings are to be accepted and we are to be blessed of God, we must learn to give freely. Jesus says, *Freely ye have received, freely give* (Matthew 10:8).

This accepting responsibility for giving freely was what prompted God to charge Moses: *Speak unto the children of Israel, that they bring me an offering: of every man that giveth it willingly with his heart ye shall take my offering* (Exodus 25:2). God was not willing to accept gifts from the people who did not want to give freely. It was this attitude that prompted Ezra to say, *And I said unto them, Ye are holy unto the Lord; the vessels are holy also; and the silver and the gold are a freewill offering unto the Lord God of your fathers* (Ezra 8:28).

Give Cheerfully

Tied closely to giving freely is the admonition that our offerings only count if we give cheerfully.

George Mueller stands as the classic example of trusting God to provide for financial needs. During the years of serving His Creator, George refused to tell any man of his needs. He felt the problem of provision was God's. And, it worked. In his huge orphanage no one ever missed a meal and God always provided remarkable miracles, sometimes at the last moment.

But one aspect of Dr. Mueller's work not many know is that he often returned offerings to people when he thought they had given unworthily. The great preacher believed it was as important "how" we give as to "what" we give or "that" we give. God's Word bears out the truth of this belief.

If our offerings are to bring dividends then we are to give cheerfully. Paul talks frankly to the church at Corinth about their giving. He says, *So I have asked these other brothers to arrive ahead of me to see that the gift you promised is on hand and waiting. I want it to be a real gift and not look as if it were being given under pressure. But remember this — if you give little, you will get little. A farmer who plants just a few seeds will get only a small crop, but if he plants much, he will reap much. Everyone must make up his own mind as to how much he should give. Don't force anyone to give more than he really wants to, for cheerful givers are the ones God prizes. God is able to make it up to you by giving you everything you need and more, so that there will not only be enough for your own needs, but plenty left over to give joyfully to others. It is as the Scripture says: "The godly man gives generously to the poor. His good deeds will be an honor to him forever."*

Continuing in the same vein, Paul adds, *For God who gives seed to the farmer to plant, and later on, good crops to harvest and eat, will give you more and more seeds to plant and will make it grow so that you can give away more and more fruit from your harvest.*

Yes, Paul insists, *God will give you much so you can give away much, and when we take your gifts to those who need them they will break out into thanksgiving and praise to God for your help. So, two good things happen as a result of your gifts — those in need are helped, and they overflow with thanks to God. Those you help will be glad not only because of your generous gifts to themselves and to others, but they will praise God for this proof that your deeds are as good as your doctrine. And they will pray for you with deep fervor and feeling because of the wonderful grace of God shown through you* (II Corinthians 9:5-14, Living Bible).

When the people of ancient Israel gave cheerfully so the Temple of the Lord could be built, it moved the heart of God and also of King David. The Bible says, *Then the people rejoiced, for that they offered willingly . . . to the Lord: and David the King also rejoiced with great joy* (I Chronicles 29:9).

From all this we learn that giving alone is not enough, just as throwing the seed in the ground carelessly is not enough for the farmer to prosper. There must be cultivation and care if the harvest is to come. So we learn that we must give

- according to our ability,
- without fanfare,
- simply,
- regularly,
- freely,
- cheerfully.

When we do, God pours out prosperity upon us.

12

How and Where to Invest Your Money

"I will probably hang onto my diamonds through almost anything," says Howard Ruff in his "Ruff recommendations" concerning his predicted money crisis. His strategy to become "panic proof" during hard times is to sock away resources in jewelry, silver, and gold coins. Real estate in smaller American towns is also good to have, he says. But, Ruff's favorite investment assurance seems to be that bit of carbon known as a woman's best friend.

Admittedly, I am a preacher not an economist. Ruff's recommendations may be wise and a good hedge against inflation, but there is one thing I am very sure about. That is that the greatest investment of our dollars we can ever make is in the Kingdom of God. If indeed God is our source, then our money is far safer with Him than in some safety deposit box disguised as jewelry or gold coins. That is why we need to learn God's rules for investing in His Kingdom and find out how to get started.

Wayne Galvin, a good friend and fine scholar from Seattle, has helped me very much to grasp the principles of God's investment program. He says, "An understanding of God's word on the subject of giving is a basic ingredient of a fruitful Christian life. Generally, however, this important aspect of Christian living is not well understood. As a result many are missing the fullness of God's blessing, and suffering financial frustration." He then shared with me the following suggestions.

Three Methods of Investment

Understanding certain methods and obeying them will allow us to reap maximum personal benefit from our giving. And at the same time our giving will provide funds for the church to carry forward the work of Christ, without resorting to worldly means or protracted appeals. The three best methods of investment are tithes, offerings, and alms. Often these terms are interchangeable, especially tithes and offerings, but such usage is not scriptural. Note that King Hezekiah brought *the offerings and the tithes* into the house of the Lord (II Chronicles 31:11, 12). The grammatical construction here shows that these two terms represent two separate entities. Also, Paul states one of his reasons for returning to Jerusalem was *to bring alms to my nation and offerings* (Acts 24:17). Again note the distinction between "alms and offerings."

Tithes are not offerings; alms are not offerings; tithes are not alms; nor are alms, tithes. These three rather are separate means of giving in the plan of God.

The Tithe

The word "tithe" represents three different words in the original text — two in the Old Testament, one in the New Testament.

In general, all three words carry the same meaning, therefore, using a single English word in translation is legitimate. All three mean "to take out," "to set aside," or "to receive one-tenth part of a whole."

The first mention of tithe is where Abraham pays tithes to Melchizedek, high priest of Salem (Genesis 14). This shows tithing antidated Israel and the Law. Jacob promised God one-tenth (a tithe) of all his increase (Genesis 28:22). And in Israel's Law we learn that all manner of produce was to be tithed: the seed, crops, fruit of the trees, herds, and flocks. Every tenth animal was to be dedicated to God regardless of its condition. If the distance to the temple was great, then the actual tithe could be exchanged for money which was easier to transport.

God's Word also tells us God did not institute tithing as an imposition or burden but rather to provide, first, a ministry to everyone regardless of their position in life. More importantly, tithes were a means of grace whereby God would return blessings to our lives because of our obedience to His word. Tithing was also a means of financial support for God's work in this world. It was seen as an ordinance and institution of God, as valid as water baptism and important to the spiritual health of the believer.

Tithing is really ROI, or "Return On Investment." No one thinks twice about paying interest to a bank on money the bank has loaned him. It is much the same with the tithe. God has invested a great deal in us. In fact, God describes us as a *peculiar people* (I Peter 2:9). This world "peculiar" is often misunderstood, it does not mean "funny" or "odd," it means "expensive!" Is it strange then that God might expect a return of one-tenth to His work, as interest on His investment in us?

The question of how often we should tithe is settled by the apostle Paul. He says we are to set aside as God prospers us (I Corinthians 16:2). Again the reference is similar to a return on investment. We are to give to God as we receive our wages, through our tithe, regularly.

Another important point to remember is that "tithe" is *one-tenth of all our produce* for any given period of time. In most cases it will simply be money. Christians who feel they cannot afford to tithe will always find themselves financially frustrated, or in a money-bind. Moreover, if a person will not tithe when earning little, he won't when earning much. It is our attitude, not the amount of money available, that makes the difference.

The Offering

In Scripture the term "offering" is always used in connection with, or in reference to, a sacrifice. This connection is so strong we often say our offering is a "sacrifice." Sacrificial offerings were and are entirely different from the tithe.

Offerings are additional, meant to meet a specific need.

In the Old Testament, God ordained offerings as a means of

cleansing from sin. Thereby, He established offerings as another means of grace. Offerings also predated Israel and the Mosaic Law.

Although offerings were ordained by God for our need, the mere act of making an offering is not enough. Often, God refused to honor an offering. It was so in the case of Cain (Genesis 4:3-5). The writer of Hebrews tells us God's acceptance of Abel's offering was a witness to Abel's righteousness and his right standing before God (Hebrews 11:4). Abel's attitude was God-centered, and thus he brought an acceptable offering to God. Cain, on the other hand, was rejected because he was self-centered and self-righteous in attitude. When he brought "the fruit of his own works," it was not accepted by God. Our attitude is of prime importance if our gifts are to be accepted by our heavenly Father.

Cain's problem was complex. The Bible suggests that God told Cain three significant things. First, Cain's basic problem was sin. Second, the situation was not irreversible, and third, if Cain would do right, not only would God accept him, but that he would regain the respect of Abel as well. But Cain would not listen.

As the older son, Cain deserved and wanted Abel's respect, but because of his self-centered, self-righteous attitude he could not obtain it. This bad attitude finally led him to murder Abel. Cain's improper attitude resulted in an improper action toward God — bringing an unacceptable offering — and God rejected him. When the pressure mounted, this bad attitude toward God resulted in an improper action toward his fellowman.

If our offerings are to be accepted, not only should our attitude toward God be right, but it is equally important that we have a clear conscience toward our fellowman as well. This is why Jesus said, *So if you are standing before the altar in the Temple, offering a sacrifice to God, and suddenly remember that a friend has something against you, leave your sacrifice there beside the altar and go and apologize and be reconciled to him, and then come and offer your sacrifice to God* (Matthew 5:23,24, Living Bible).

To recognize the significance of an offering as a sacrifice we need to know something about sacrifice. A sacrifice is defined as some action that is unusual, something that carries some sort of a personal price tag. When the Israelite brought an offering from his flock, it was to be the very best (II Samuel 24:24). David declared he would not offer to God that which cost him nothing.

Remember too, the story of the widow's mite. Jesus stood and watched how the worshipers cast their money into the treasury, and when He saw the widow cast in her two mites, He said, *This poor widow hath cast in more than they all* (Luke 21:3). It wasn't "more than anyone," but "more than they all!" This poor widow's pittance amounted to greater value in God's sight than the entire sum made by all others. This simple story shows God values our offerings by the personal cost and attitude of the giver.

God told Israel He would not accept their offerings since they were of small value to them, and because their attitudes were wrong in giving (Malachi 1:7-14). Just because we make an offering does not automatically oblige God to accept it. To be acceptable an offering should meet three conditions:

- It must be accompanied by a right attitude toward God. We must sincerely desire to make the offering, prompted by love for God and His work, not merely as a religious "duty" or a desire for reward.
- Our offering must be accompanied by a right attitude toward our fellowman. That is, we should be innocent of any offence which will inhibit the work of God in another person's life.
- Our offering should be in some measure a sacrifice. That is, we have put aside some personal desire, or assumed a more humble position in life in order to advance the work of the Lord.

A deeper study of giving reveals another term used in the New Testament. It is "gift." The New Testament offering is a "gift to God." It is a sacrifice made voluntarily on our part on behalf of the Kingdom of God.

In review we learn that an offering is something above and beyond our usual tithe. It has some personal "price tag" for the giver and it is given or done to meet a special or a specific need.

Also, it is a gift from us to God. Finally, it should be accompanied by a right attitude toward both God and our fellowman.

Alms Giving

The giving of alms is probably the least understood and most frequently overlooked of the three methods. In the English Bible, alms is a New Testament term exclusively, but it is used frequently in the LXX or Septuagint translation of the Old Testament. The term may be relatively contemporary, but the actions implied are at least as old as Israel.

Because alms does not have the obvious emphasis accorded to tithes and offerings, it has not been given equal prominence in the Christian life. This is tragic, since God intends His ministry to the poor as a means of bringing unbelievers into fellowship with His people to hear the Gospel. Because of our default, the function of this ministry has been assumed by the government, and is now nearly lost to the church — yet welfare started with God.

God emphasizes the importance of alms in a most unique way. This emphasis is given in the account of the conversion of Cornelius. Reading Luke's account (Acts 10) we see Cornelius is told by an angel of God that his "alms" were *come up for a memorial before God.* This same declaration is repeated, *thine alms are had in remembrance in the sight of God.* Real emphasis and importance is given to this ministry of alms. They were a memorial in the sight of God. God took special notice of them and made an everlasting record of the alms of Cornelius. It is even more amazing to realize there is no comparably strong statement made regarding tithes or offerings. Thus, we must conclude that in God's sight, alms are at least equally as important as tithes and offerings.

"Just what is alms?" we might ask. The Greek word for alms means "compassion." However, this definition is not near enough. In the Septuagint we find the word alms used to interpret an Old Testament term for "righteousness," as it related to the act of doing good, or relieving the oppressed, or of giving to the poor. Alms is used similarly in the New Testament account of the lame man who sat at the temple gate called Beautiful. He was begging money or *an alms* of those entering (Acts 3:2, 3).

For the Israelite, giving money to the poor was an act of righteousness. It still is for us, if done in the proper manner and with the right attitude. But the Jews forgot the proper, God-honoring method, and began to make a big show of giving to the poor. It became, at last, a kind of parade. The Pharisees would go to the houses of the poor, preceded by musicians and a crier who would shout, "Make way! Make way! Pharisee Simon comes to give an alms to the widow!" Then Simon would appear, richly garbed, pleased to acknowledge the applause and praise of his audience.

This was the sort of vain demonstration to which Jesus referred when he told them sharply, *Take heed that ye do not your alms before men, to be seen of them: otherwise ye have no reward of your Father which is in heaven. Therefore when thou doest thine alms, do not sound a trumpet before thee, as the hypocrites do in the synagogues and in the streets, that they may have glory of men. Verily I say unto you, They have their reward. But when thou doest alms, let not thy left hand know what thy right hand doeth* (Matthew 6:1-4).

Alms giving, therefore, is a personal gift from ourselves to someone in need. It is to be accomplished in a quiet manner, as unto God. Such gifts need not be in the form of money. Luke refers to almsdeeds (Acts 9:36). This was an activity performed on behalf of a person in need. It was a helping hand at the right moment. It could be a gift of cash, or clothing, or food. Our Lord tells us that not even a cup of cold water given in His name will pass the notice of God.

Alms are also over and above our tithe. The personal gift or deed is to be performed quietly, without partiality, concern for reward, or the recognition of men. Most importantly it is to be done in a compassionate manner, not demanding to the recipient. This final qualification is where most state agencies fail.

God has instituted three methods of giving for His people. Furthermore, these three are not independent of one another. Rather, each adds to the other to provide a complete financial involvement for the work of God in this world.

- Tithe is to meet the general needs of the church. It is a

definite portion of our substance, and should be ministered regularly as we receive our wages. It should go to our church or "storehouse," where we get our spiritual food.

- Offerings are to meet special needs, over and above our regular tithe. An offering is not necessarily money, but is ministered as a need is made known. It is a personal gift direct from ourselves to God. God can tell us where to give these offerings.
- Alms, like offerings, are also to meet special needs, over and above our regular tithe. They are not necessarily money and are ministered as the opportunity presents itself. Unlike offerings, however, alms are a personal gift given directly from us to our fellowman in the love and name of Christ.

Of the three methods of investment, tithes seem to be the most difficult to handle for most people. There is a basic reason for this difficulty. That is because God has ordained the tithe as the financial mainstay of His church. Satan does his utmost to cause us to disregard this method. He does it by trying to keep us ignorant of God's Word on the subject, by depreciating the need, by inflating the value of the money in our minds, and finally causing us to forget the true nature of the tithe and its real value to us as a means of blessing.

Those who feel that they cannot afford to tithe are looking only at one side of their coin. The other side is whether they can afford to miss any of God's blessings in their lives, their families, or their businesses. It is not that God withholds a blessing, but rather that He cannot add *further* blessing apart from our action.

We need to remember that whenever God provides a method of bringing His blessings to our lives, He also provides the means necessary for us to obtain those blessings.

As we respond to God's methods of giving we will find that He will also supply the means in a more than adequate measure. However, as with salvation, the means do not precede but follow our response. The question is not whether we can afford to give to God, but whether we can afford not to give to God.

While working my way through college I rode in a car pool with other believers. Quite often the subject of tithing would come up. One of the men was most adamant about how tithing was an Old

Testament commandment and not for us today. No amount of reasoning would change his mind. Finally, we just gave up on him and let him have his way. But the most tragic part of that story is that through the years all of us who paid our tithes have prospered, but my adamant friend is still struggling to pay his bills, and laboring under heavy debt. He has struggled spiritually, physically, and financially. It seems as soon as he can see the light, something else will happen to his family such as a sickness, an accident or a problem with the car or house. The price of disobedience is high.

After several years in "the living laboratory of human experience" I have discovered that people who do not pay their tithes, give their offerings, and participate in almsgiving, should not necessarily be condemned; they should be pitied. They are taking food from the mouths of their children. They are gambling with the health and safety of their loved ones. Malachi was right when he said, *Bring all your tithes into the storehouse so that there will be food enough in my Temple; if you do, I will open up the windows of heaven for you and pour out a blessing so great you won't have room enough to take it in!*

Malachi continues, *"Try it! Let me prove it to you! Your crops will be large, for I will guard them from insects and plagues. Your grapes won't shrivel away before they ripen," says the Lord of Hosts. "And all nations will call you blessed, for you will be a land sparkling with happiness. These are the promises of the Lord of Hosts* (Malachi 3:10-12, Living Bible).

Before we leave this important subject we should mention that this is the only promise of God where He tells us to try it out and see if it works! With all his other promises He tells us to believe them and He will prove them. But this one He says we can prove before we have to believe it. I don't know about you, but I want to take God up on His challenge.

13

Insurance for the Future

Man has long tried to anchor himself in the choppy and uncertain waters of life. One of the earliest attempts to do so is still with us; insurance. The idea of insurance can be traced back to the Book of Genesis where Joseph set aside reserves for the coming bad years. Later many other cultures adopted their own plans to do the same.

The Code of Hammuali, a collection of Babylonian laws written seventeen hundred years before Christ, introduced the first known form of credit insurance. Under its provision the borrower was not held responsible if personal misfortune made repayment impossible. Of course, the borrower paid extra for this provision in addition to his regular rate of interest.

In Roman times even slaves and wage earners could purchase life insurance with such benefits as burial costs, old age pensions, and disability protection. Guilds formed by various craftsmen of the Middle Ages offered not only life insurance, but also protection for property against fire and theft.

Marine insurance began at Lloyd's coffeehouse in England during the late 1600s, when the technique of underwriting was born. A statement of the ship's cargo was recorded on a slip of paper and persons willing to share the risk of insuring the cargo would sign their names under it. Each would indicate the share of the load he wanted to guarantee. If things went well, he was paid handsomely for his gamble.

Then modern fire insurance came as a direct result of the great fire of London in 1666.

Benjamin Franklin introduced insurance to the new world by forming the first life and fire insurance companies in 1752 and 1759. Both companies are still in existence and are doing very well.

Insurance companies have grown into vast financial empires with sophisticated computers and actuality charts. It is even now possible to buy all kinds of protection from insuring a musician's hands, a singer's voice or an actor's nose or legs. Today even pet insurance is available giving the owner compensation from accidents. (Dog insurance uses nose prints to identify the insured animal and the policy covers all hazards except poisoning.)

Yet, in spite of all his insurance plans, man is still insecure. The obvious reason is that the protection he needs and seeks cannot come from a human source. Only a divine heavenly Father can provide that need. And, in that provision perhaps one of the clearest and most succinct insurance policies in the world is found in Psalm 37. If a man has every earthly policy available but not this one, he is horribly underinsured. Far greater than any earthly policy, the psalmist's plan offers peace, protection, and provision. And the premiums are very small.

Peace of Mind

Charles Schultz captures the basic needs and foibles of mankind in his interesting comic strip, "Peanuts." One of the star characters, Linus, is bound to his "security blanket." His life is shattered without that blanket and he cannot leave it.

Man has a great need for security. In fact, when our lifestyle changes, severe emotional and physical problems can develop because our security is challenged. It has long been known that when a life mate dies, the remaining marriage partner becomes extremely vulnerable to emotional and even physical illness. It is not surprising when the one who is left dies within a matter of weeks or months. His security has been disturbed and the result is often so devastating it is life threatening. The same vulnerability can happen with a man's change of job and retirement, or a mother's family growing up and away from her.

One of the reasons why adultery is so destructive to the human being is that it disturbs a family's security. Unnatural rivalry is introduced into the marriage relationship and hardly any union can survive continued interruption of security. Man craves and desperately needs peace of mind, but God has never created a need in man without doing something about it. The psalmist tells us what that something is.

David notes, *But the meek shall inherit the earth; and shall delight themselves in the abundance of peace* (Psalm 37:11). Peace in a warring world seems elusive, at least to the nonbeliever. However, God has promised peace to those who follow Him. Isaiah promised, *And the work of righteousness shall be peace; the effect of righteousness quietness and assurance for ever. And my people shall dwell in peaceable habitation, and in sure dwellings, and in quiet resting places* (Isaiah 32:17, 18).

When a person comes to Christ he comes to know peace. The tensions drain from his life and his relationships with others stabilize. This is why Isaiah also said, *And wisdom and knowledge shall be the stability of thy times, and strength of salvation: the fear of the Lord is his treasure* (Isaiah 33:6). There is no real peace in a life outside of the "Prince of Peace."

Sin keeps a person and family torn up. Rivalries, rights, and irresponsibility in relationships result from the sin of selfishness. Sin most simply defined is, "I want what I want, when I want it." There is little peace in living with a person like that, whether it be a mate or ourselves. That is why Isaiah notes: *But the wicked are like the troubled sea, when it cannot rest, whose waters cast up mire and dirt. There is no peace, saith my God, to the wicked* (Isaiah 57:20, 21).

It is true that those who do not follow Christ can sometimes give an appearance of peace. But, to do so they often have to anesthetize themselves with pills or liquor. It is much like a swimmer who plays with a large beach ball. As long as he pays attention to that ball he can keep it under water. But, the moment the swimmer diverts his attention elsewhere that ball explodes upward. So, an evil person can keep himself in control at times, but, at some point of inattention there will be an explosion, an eruption of bitter anger and emotions that can destroy those about him.

Real peace can only be found in a relationship with God. David's insurance policy assures peace. In fact he boldly claims, *Mark the perfect man, and behold the upright: for the end of that man is peace* (Psalm 37:37). There is also another fantastic aspect of David's unusual policy.

Protection

Irwin Shaw wrote a provocative book entitled *Rich Man, Poor Man,* and then another, *Beggarman, Thief.* The two books tell the story of the Jordache family and follow the various members through their trials and triumphs. The elder brother rises to great riches, yet his personal life falls apart. Commenting on this, one of the book's characters says of his wealth and power, "He had all that protection, yet he still got hurt."

Man simply cannot build his walls high enough to protect himself from hurt. Protection — emotionally, spiritually and physically — can only come from God — and in David's insurance policy God promises and provides such protection. There are specific clauses where he promises to justify us, uphold us, give us strength to meet trouble, and lift us when we fall.

David knew that defending himself against the accusations of his enemies was a never ending and debilitating experience. That is why he says in Psalm 37 it is much better to let God justify us and our decisions. *And he shall bring forth thy righteousness as the light, and thy judgment as the noonday* (verse 6). As our defender, God will prove to the world both our righteousness and the rightness of decisions we make in crisis.

He also upholds us through trying times: *For the arms of the wicked shall be broken: but the Lord upholdeth the righteous* (verse 17).

Knowing that troubles come to all men, God promises in this policy, *But the salvation of the righteous is of the Lord: he is their strength in time of trouble* (verse 39). Again, *And the Lord shall help them and . . . deliver them from the wicked, and save them, because they trust in him* (verse 40).

But God also knows that we all have a downward pull. Each one of us has an Achilles' heel and is vulnerable in some way. Therefore, when we fail, and all of us will at some time, there is a precious promise: *The steps of a good man are ordered by the Lord: and he delighteth in his way. Though he fall, he shall not be utterly cast down: for the Lord upholdeth him with his hand* (verses 23, 24).

Karl A. Menninger, a great psychiatrist, talked often about the times of crisis that come commonly to all men. He says, "When a trout rising to a fly gets hooked and finds himself unable to swim around freely, he begins a fight which results in struggles and splashes and sometimes an escape. . . In the same way, the human being struggles . . . with hooks that catch him. Sometimes he masters his difficulties; sometimes they are too much for him. His struggles are all the world can see and it usually misunderstands them. It is hard for a free fish to understand what is happening to a hooked one."

These are no doubt wise words. However, on the premise of the promise in Psalm 37, we would amend that — when we are hooked, God will set us free. More than that — after we have been hooked and freed by God we can indeed understand what our fellow "hooked" fish are experiencing. Peter could easily identify with those who failed after his own bitter and soul-shattering experience.

So the promise is for protection. And if we get hooked on one of the vicissitudes of life, God will deliver us and strengthen us through it. Just recently a broken ex-minister sat in my office and shared his shame of defeat. His broken life had disappointed God and shattered his family. As we talked and shared the promises of God's Word he began to see that what the world calls defeat can become bright victory to the believer. Defeat shows us that *without* Christ we are ugly and miserable, but *with* Christ we can live as victors. My minister friend will fly again; the promise from God's Word is that his latter days will be even brighter and greater than his former. God specializes in failures. We only need to remember Moses, Mark, and Peter to understand that. But there is more!

Provision

In our spiraling inflationary period of history perhaps one of the most precious of the promises in this unusual insurance policy is that of provision.

After seeing the deprivation and disaster of India I returned home with a new awareness of life's real values and a new perspective to my devotional Bible reading. One of the verses that began to disturb me for the first time was, *I have been young, and now am old; yet have I not seen the righteous forsaken, nor his seed begging bread* (Psalm 37:25).

Living on this side of the ocean I had never given much thought to that Scripture and freely admitted that I too had never seen His seed begging bread. But India disturbed me. Over 60 percent of that land has hungry and dying people. While collectively Americans are 2.3 billions of pounds overweight, Indians rarely know what a full stomach is. Could this Scripture be true in India? It was a haunting question that demanded an honest answer.

For several months I fretted over the question. The Scripture dropped out of my sermons because I never want to preach anything that seems like "glossed over truth." Oh, I believed it, because I believe God's Word. But I had to know whether in the living laboratory of human sorrow, it worked.

Finally, Mark Buntain came back to America for special meetings. We were scheduled to appear together on a national television program and were staying at the same guest house. I asked him the question. His answer still moves me.

Mark said, "Ron, I have been asked that question many times. I can honestly say that in all my twenty-five years in Calcutta — the world's most desperate city — I have never found one Christian who has starved or begged. I have found some who had an awareness of Christianity and maybe were raised in a church, who have suffered hunger. But, I have never once in all my years discovered a faithful believer whose needs were not being met by our Lord. I can report the Scripture is still true."

In Psalm 37 David says that God will provide for our needs. These include a place to live: *Trust in the Lord and do good, so shalt thou dwell in the land;* food: . . . *and be fed* (verse 3), and financial resources: *The Lord knoweth the days of the upright: and their inheritance shall be for ever. They shall not be ashamed in the evil time: and in the days of famine they shall be satisfied* (verses 18, 19).

Isaiah uses a colorful word picture to reinforce David's note, *And I will fasten him as a nail in a sure place* (Isaiah 22:23). This great promise to Eliakim can certainly be applied to our lives. We are secure in that.

So there we have it. God's insurance policy contains assurances for peace, protection, and provision. But, there is a cost. As we have already learned, "there ain't no such thing as a free lunch." God's contract has terms.

Terms of the Policy

The first cost is commitment. We have already learned that God does not hear or answer the prayers of the unrighteous. Jeremiah notes: *but my people have changed their glory for that which doth not profit* (Jeremiah 2:11). This policy is reserved exclusively for those who follow our God.

The first step in signing up is, *That if thou shalt confess with thy mouth the Lord Jesus, and believe in thine heart that God hath raised him from the dead, thou shalt be saved* (Romans 10:9). Then, after this initial step there are some attitudes and action God wants us to practice. These are all outlined carefully in Psalm 37 so there will be no misunderstanding of the terms.

I have underlined these clauses in my Bible. Perhaps you will want to do the same. They are:

1) *Fret not thyself* (verse 1). In other words, don't worry about things you have no control over. Jesus gave us a commandment, *Let not your heart be troubled* (John 14:1). Worry is a habit of spirit and like John, Haggai so eloquently says, "To worry is to insult your God."
2) *Trust . . . and do good* (verse 3). Our faith is active. We lean on God and we develop healthy patterns in attitudes and actions. The combination is "Trust and Do." We can no more "trust" and not "do" as we can "do" and not "trust."

3) *Delight thyself* (verse 4). Relax, and remember that God's plan for your life is far more exciting than your own. His vision is bigger than yours. You give up little to come to him. In fact it is *ashes you exchange for beauty, joy you get for your mourning, and praise for your depression* (Isaiah 61:3). Not a bad trade in any marketplace.
4) *Commit thy way* (verse 5). Remember God is the author and finisher of your faith. When we are committed to Him we need to trust Him enough to know He will bring us through, and bring His plans for us to pass. God assured Jeremiah, *For thou shalt go to all that I shall send thee, and whatsoever I command thee thou shalt speak* (Jeremiah 1:7). God's commandments are God's enablements.
5) *Rest . . . and wait* (verse 7). Perhaps this is the hardest piece of advice for aggressive people to follow. Like Abraham, we always try to help God out. But, I suspect He knows exactly the best time for His works. That's why Habakkuk quotes God saying, *Write my answer on a billboard, large and clear, so that anyone can read it at a glance and rush to tell the others."* God continues, *But these things I plan won't happen right away. Slowly, steadily, surely, the time approaches when the vision will be fulfilled. If it seems slow, do not despair, for these things will surely come to pass. Just be patient! They will not be overdue a single day!"* (Habakkuk 2:2, 3, Living Bible).
6) *Keep His way* (verse 34). We have to play by God's rules. We can't win any sporting game by cheating all the time, nor can we hope to have His insurance policy unless we are truly committed to Christ. There is no such thing as being a little committed to Christ any more than there is such a thing as being a little bit pregnant. You either are or you aren't. We either keep His way or your own way. As Billy Sunday said, "There is no such thing as a 'heavenly devil' and no such thing as a 'worldly Christian.' "
7) *Cease from anger* (verse 8). Most of us get angry on occasion. Sometimes we don't even recognize the origin of our anger but it leads to depression and can precipitate destruction. God's Word tells us to defuse our anger through forgiveness. We should let God take care of those who hurt us. Booker T. Washington said

at one time, "I will permit no man to reduce my soul to the level of hatred." This is why God's Word says, *Now your attitudes and thoughts must all be constantly changing for the better. Yes, you must be a new and different person, holy and good. Clothe yourself with this new nature . . . If you are angry, don't sin by nursing your grudge. Don't let the sun go down with you still angry—get over it quickly; for when you are angry you give a mighty foothold to the devil* (Ephesians 4:23-27, Living Bible).

One of the drawbacks of many insurance policies is that a person has to die before his relatives and heirs can reap the benefits. However, with the policy mentioned in Psalms, there is immediate benefit and a tremendous retirement plan. Thus, the best insurance policy we could possibly acquire is that assurance that comes from the Word of God. Any other insurance plan, however promising, is wholly inadequate to the divine one that is planned by and offered to us by our Lord. If He indeed is our source, then only He can insure us against the difficulties of life.

Paul had the policy. That is why he could confidently say, *For I am convinced that nothing can ever separate us from his love. Death can't, and life can't. The angels won't, and all the powers of hell itself cannot keep God's love away. Our fears for today, our worries about tomorrow, or where we are — high above the sky, or in the deepest ocean — nothing will ever be able to separate us from the love of God demonstrated by our Lord Jesus Christ when he died for us* (Romans 8:38, 39, Living Bible).

God's Word tells us that when we trust in people we will be disappointed (Jeremiah 17:5). When we trust in our wealth, we will fall (Proverbs 11:28). And, if we trust in ourselves, we are fools (Proverbs 28:26). But when we trust in God we will go from strength to strength.

The proverbist adds, *But the path of the just is as the shining light, that shineth more and more unto the perfect day* (Proverbs 4:18). With such promises given to us, we are staggered at God's mercy and love.

14

God's Show and Tell

"Motion pictures are a hopeless novelty and the public will never support them," so said Thomas Edison when asked about the future of that new invention.

Sir John Erichsen, celebrated British surgeon, said in 1873, "The abdomen, chest, and brain of man will forever be closed to the surgeon."

Thomas Edison forecast, "The future of the wireless telegraph does not exist."

Robcrt Fulton proclaimcd, "Wc havc found a motivc powcr in steam, but of a nature so comparatively feeble that a child's toy could hardly be put in motion by it."

Admiral William Leahy assured us in 1945, "The atom bomb will never go off."

Franklin Delano Roosevelt stated confidently in 1922, "It is highly unlikely that the airplane, or even a fleet of them, could ever successfully sink a fleet of Navy vessels under battle conditions."

Marshall Ferdinand Foch, commander in chief of the Allied Armies proclaimed flatly in 1910, "The airplane is fine for sport. But it is of no use to the army."

H.G. Wells prophesied back in 1902, "Submarines can never be more than iron coffins."

So much for the wisdom of man in his prophesies!

It would be well now to consider these fallible and foolish predictions in the light of some of the gloom perpetrated by the prophets of doom. It just might be that what they so assuredly forecast may never come to pass at all. (Although at this point in history it would appear that we are indeed heading for some financial crash.)

The one thing the economists do not realize is that long ago God said, *If my people, which are called by my name, shall humble themselves, and pray, and seek my face, and turn from their wicked ways; then will I hear from heaven, and will forgive their sin, and will heal their land* (II Chronicles 7:14). Nations have been on the brink of total collapse before and God's people have started praying. Revival has come and economies have been restored and people blessed.

The beautiful assurance for the believer is that God's promises take and hold shape during bad times as well as good. It makes no difference what the conditions are since God is our source. We are not victimized by conditions, but rather we are victorious over them. God wants a vibrant and victorious people.

Paul the apostle tells us why God wishes us success: *I should preach among the Gentiles the unsearchable riches of Christ; And to make all men see what is the fellowship of the mystery which from the beginning of the world hath been hid in God, who created all things by Jesus Christ: To the intent that now unto the principalities and powers in heavenly places might be known by the church the manifold wisdom of God* (Ephesians 3:8-10). In other words the Bible says that our lives have been put in God's test-tube to prove to the world that it pays to serve God.

This premise should not surprise us. From the beginning God said it would be so. Note what God tells Israel: *But against any of the children of Israel shall not a dog move his tongue, against man or beast: that ye may know how that the Lord doth put a difference between the Egyptians and Israel* (Exodus 11:7). Thus we see that we are God's "show and tell." He loves this world so deeply that he has created us so we can show each other that it pays to serve God. Our lives of real prosperity are to reflect how He is perfectly able to keep us in all time, whether good or evil.

Paul picks up on this premise a number of times saying, *That we should be to the praise of his glory . . .* (Ephesians 1:12). And, according to Paul, God proves not only to the world that it pays to serve God, but also our lives prove this to the power and principalities of all the universe. This earth is a proving grounds of righteousness and truth. This is exactly why, *Let them shout for joy, and be glad, that favour my righteous cause: yea, let them say continually, Let the Lord be magnified, which hath pleasure in the prosperity of his servant* (Psalm 35:27).

The bad times may or may not come, but regardless of the way the wind blows the Christian should not be disturbed. God has promised prosperity regardless of the economic condition of a society. God's promises do not rise and fall with the consumer index. Similarly, our emotions should not rise or fall with the cash flow of our company or of our personal financial accounts.

I have thought much about Howard Ruff's recommendations in his popular book, *How to Prosper in the Coming Bad Years.* Something about them deeply disturbs me. I suppose it is because the premise is advanced that we are the masters of our fates and the captains of our souls. That argument was long ago abandoned by the rational humanists who found that it never really did work. Man may prepare and hoard, but God says in His Word that He can "blow upon it" and it will vanish.

I think of a little lady God spoke to during a recent missions convention. The woman's pastor had engaged a missionary who challenged the widow's heart. During the morning service God impressed her to give to the missionary the few hundred dollars she had saved in her bank for coming "rainy days." She argued with God, since she was so alone in the world, and left the service without obeying the impression.

A few days later the woman called her pastor and asked him to come to her house. When he did she handed him a check for all that was in her bank account, to be given to the missionary. The pastor argued with her saying he was not sure she should deplete her resources, even though the cause to which she was giving was indeed worthy.

"Pastor," the woman said through her tears, "Please don't cheat me of a blessing. You see, after Sunday, the Lord would not let me rest. I prayed a lot about the matter and one night our Lord impressed me that what I had hoarded in preparation for bad times was not nearly enough to meet those needs. My little savings account would be wiped out by even the slightest sickness. At that moment I knew He wanted me to throw all my trust on Him and He would take care of me. Please take the check."

The pastor did and then sat back to see if God would keep His Word. Of course He did. Although this woman had no relatives the Lord provided her with a better and bigger home within one year of her gift. Not only that but she has ever since enjoyed the best health of her life. Her fear of future financial disaster is gone and she is more relaxed, more loving, and a happier, healthier person. She has learned the secret of depending solely on God.

Now I am not suggesting that you go out and give away all your savings; I am not telling you to sell your property and send your resources to some religious organization, but I will say that you might just find that if you rely on your own resources more than on those of our heavenly Father, that He will ask you to dispose of them. After all, is this not what he asked of the rich young ruler? God never intends for our possessions to possess us. We are to trust Him — not the "work of our own hands." One of the strongest reasons for tithing is to be reminded each week that we are stewards of the earth's resources — not owners.

Without doubt it is this concept that bothers me about Ruff's recommendations. Perhaps he would disagree with my criticism, saying I had misinterpreted his motives, his book and its plans. But, still I am bothered. Ruff says there are basically five things we should do to prepare for the bad times. They are:

1) Store up food for your family so in the event of a crisis you could survive for a full year. This suggestion sounds good and many Christians are doing just that. Frankly, I have difficulty in reconciling this with what our Lord says: *Don't worry about things — food, drink and clothes. For you already have life and a body — and they are far more important than what to eat and wear. Look at the birds! They don't worry about what to eat — they don't need to sow or reap or store up food — for your heavenly Father feeds them. And you are far more valuable to*

him than they are. Will all your worries add a single moment to your life?

Jesus continues, *And why worry about your clothes? Look at the field lilies! They don't worry about theirs. Yet King Solomon in all his glory was not clothed as beautifully as they. And if God cares so wonderfully for flowers that are here today and gone tomorrow, won't he more surely care for you, O men of little faith?*

So don't worry at all, Jesus insists, *about having enough food and clothing. Why be like the heathen? For they take pride in all these things and are deeply concerned about them. But your heavenly Father already knows perfectly well that you need them, and he will give them to you if you give him first place in your life and live as He wants you to* (Matthew 6:25-33, Living Bible).

2) Buy silver and gold coins as a safety against paper money and as a hedge against inflation. Ruff's fear that our dollar is rapidly deteriorating is a sound one. However, God desires that we trust Him rather than our dollars. *Don't store up treasures,* Jesus says, *where they can erode away or may be stolen. Store them in heaven where they will never lose their value, and are safe from thieves. If your profits are in heaven your heart will be there too* (Matthew 6:19-21, Living Bible).

3) Avoid unsound debt, while using sound leverage for safety and profit. These suggestions sound excellent. However, there is an attitude problem here too. Ruff recommends eliminating consumer debts, as we do, but then he goes on to say, have enough money in the bank to assure that we can pay the loans we do have for a year. He also says not to lend money to anyone except a friend in need. We have already learned that it is best not to "owe" anyone anything but love, then we learned that Christ tells us to "lend" to those in need. I agree with all this except the cash reserves. The attitude problem that disturbs me is his suggestion of storing up money fearing some future crisis. Jesus says, *So don't be anxious about tomorrow. God will take care of your tomorrow too. Live one day at a time* (Matthew 6:34, Living Bible).

4) Sell or trade all big city and suburban real estate to invest in small town property. Ruff's idea here is that when the crisis comes, the best protection for your safety is in the smaller community. The cities, he says, will become virtual battlegrounds where there is no safety. Again the attitude of this suggestion bothers me because I know our safety is not in a place, but a person — Jesus Christ. Jesus said, *Don't be afraid of those who can kill only your bodies — but can't touch your souls! Fear only God who can destroy both soul and body in hell. Not one sparrow (What do they cost? Two for a penny?) can fall to the ground without your father knowing it. And the very hairs of your head are numbered. So don't worry! You are more valuable to him than many sparrows* (Matthew 10:28-31, Living Bible).

5) Prepare for price controls and a black market inflationary economy. Ruff's complicated suggestions here are to buy up mass-produced foods for storage and bartering. He says you are to improve your survival education and purchase needed clothing for the coming crunch. He also suggests preparing for energy needs through alternate forms of energy or by hoarding gasoline and oil. Again the problem is depending on ourselves as the source, rather than on God. The best Scripture to answer this includes the whole first Psalm.

My good friend Bill Garwaith, producer of the famed PTL Club, says the first Psalm is such a dramatic promise that he has accepted it as God's personal check to him. As evidence of Bill's faith he has signed his own name at the bottom of Psalm One endorsing the check. And, God has honored Bill's faith. Note what the Psalmist says:

> *Oh, the joys of those who do not follow evil men's advice, who do not hang around with sinners, scoffing at the things of God: But they delight in doing everything God wants them to, and day and night are always meditating on his laws and thinking about ways to follow him more closely.*
>
> *They are like trees along a river bank bearing luscious fruit each season without fail. Their leaves shall never wither, and all they do shall prosper.*

But for sinners, what a different story! They blow away like chaff before the wind. They are not safe on Judgment Day; they shall not stand among the godly.

For the Lord watches over all the plans and paths of godly men, but the paths of the godless lead to doom.

(Living Bible)

Standing in stark contrast to Mr. Ruff's recommendations are those from God's Word that we have tried to include in this brief book. For emphasis and clarity let us state them again. The premises of prosperity from God's Word are:

- Knowing why God wants us to prosper. We prosper because he desires the ends of the earth to know Him and His love. Our only mission is missions.
- Want is a spiritual problem. This is why God says, *Your iniquities have turned away these things, and your sins have withholden good things from you* (Jeremiah 5:25).
- God is our source. He provides all our needs, not just the financial ones. Prosperity is more than money in the bank — rather, it is peace in the heart.
- Sin hits us in the pocketbook. All sins cost and the collective sin of our society is driving taxes sky high. But, our own petty sins have price tags to them also.
- The biggest barrier to financial success is our disobedience to the laws of God. We never successfully break His laws; we break ourselves on them.
- Misplaced values, stinginess, and laziness devour our dollars.
- Wanton pleasure, excessive appetites, and bad friends also devaluate our dollars.
- God gives us five ways to increase our income. They are obeying God, looking to God rather than our own resources, caring for the needy, being generous with our money, and paying our tithes.
- There are set principles of business success that we have to learn and follow. These deal with honesty and attitudes toward those who work for us.

• It is just as important "how" we give as it is "that" we give and "what" we give. We must also remember it is possible to give without loving, but not possible to love without giving.
• The only really effective insurance we can have in life is that which God gives through a relationship with Him.
• We are blessed financially, spiritually, and emotionally, so that we might be the "praise of His glory" and prove to the world it pays to serve God.

Karl Marx laughed at religion, calling it "the opiate of the people." Well, he was wrong. Faith in Christ is not the opiate; it is the medicine. And our world is sick. There is a sickness in our economy and in our relationships, but Christ can and will come into that sickness and heal it. All we have to do is follow the prescription in His Word for prosperity.

That is why we can confidently face the future. Ira Stanphill said it in his well known song, "I don't know what the future holds, but I know who holds the future." With such faith we can confidently affirm again that we can prosper in bad times.

Epilogue

The Sins of Sodom

Three female seamen were recently discharged from the United States Navy after an investigation into their sexual activities. The spokesman for the group said she was reported to base authorities when a male sailor came into her room and found her naked in bed with another female. The male sailor had come to the room looking for a wallet he lost during a party the night before.

"I would rather he jumped in bed with us," the discharged woman said, "Three's better than two." She added, "Everybody here is cool. We smoke dope and drink alcohol until 4 A.M. right in the barracks."

Scenes such as these, disgusting as they may be, occur with seeming increasing frequency — and it is not unique to the armed forces. Such blatant sin is a reflection of modern society and the "new morality." Without question North American society smacks of Sodom.

A careful investigation into the society of Sodom indicates problems deeper than what is immediately seen. The sexual perversion recorded in Genesis 19 is so distasteful that often we overlook the real causes of such aberrant behavior. But the Bible is very clear on what the real sins of Sodom were, and how these sins created a society that deteriorated into homosexuality and incest. Strangely enough there is a remarkable repetition of these sins in modern North American society and we too are seeing sexual perversion as a direct result. The Bible indicates sodomy and incest in Sodom were the final expression of sins that had long plagued the sister cities of Sodom and Gomorrah. Ezekiel clearly outlined those specific sins which bred moral impurity.

Ezekiel, son of a respected priestly family, preached for twenty-two years to his fellow hostages in Babylon. He had spent his early years in Jerusalem but was kidnapped with other hostages by Nebuchadnezzar. There he settled in his own house in the village of Nippur, along the banks of the Chebar. Ten years later his beloved wife died and the home on Nebuchadnezzar's royal court seemed empty. Yet he continued his faithful preaching and at the same time saw Israel sinking into deeper sin. People seemed to be adding "sin unto sin." He reminded Israel that years before he had told them punishment would come because they were repeating sins of other nations. He specifically pointed out the problem to Sodom.

Ezekiel says of Sodom: *Behold, this was the iniquity of thy sister Sodom, pride, fulness of bread, and abundance of idleness was in her and in her daughters, neither did she strengthen the hand of the poor and needy* (Ezekiel 16:49). These four basic sins created a climate of perversion and preoccupation with pleasure resulting in the sordid society of Sodom.

Pride Was Primary

Sodom's first sin was pride. Located in the lush plains, Genesis described Sodom, *even as the garden of the Lord, like the land of Egypt, as thou comest unto Zoar* (Genesis 13:10). Yet, rather than acknowledge their envied position as a gift of a loving God the Sodomites took credit for the magnificent society they had built. Rather than being deo-centric (God-centered) they became egocentric (self-centered).

Pride cuts off compassion and care. Arrogance short circuits mercy since it produces an attitude of "I made it, why can't you?"

Replacing God from the throne of our lives means replacing him with ourselves, and as we turn inward we destroy our psyche. Man was created for relationships with God and his fellowman — egocentric behavior isolates us from these relationships. That is why God hates pride. Pride destroys the ones He loves.

English Poet Percy Bysshe Shelley talked much about the futility of pride. In a poetic masterpiece entitled, "Ozymandias," he wrote:

I met a traveler from an antique land
Who said: "Two vast and trunkless legs of stone
Stand in the desert. Near them, on the sand,
Half sunk, a shattered visage lies, whose frown,
And wrinkled lip, and sneer of cold command,
Tell that its sculptor well those passions read
Which yet survive, stamped on these lifeless things,
The hand that mocked them, and the heart that fed:
And on the pedestal these words appear:
My name is Ozymandias, king of kings:
Look on my works, ye Mighty, and despair!
Nothing beside remains. Round the decay
Of that colossal wreck, boundless and bare
The lone and level sands stretch far away.
(1817; 1818)

While we are aware of pride's destructive force, still we see it in our society. As a nation we brag about being the best; we boast of our military might, and our enlightened society. Each of our athletes are encouraged to be "number one." We look on the Third World as "poor simple" people. Probably we are not all that different from Sodom and pride that brought destruction. Tragically this pride even expresses itself in religion. We compete for attention and applause, believing we are more spiritual than our other neighborhood churches. Seldom do we see Paul's admonitions acted out: *Let nothing be done through strife or vainglory: but in lowliness of mind let each esteem other better than themselves* (Philippians 2:3).

Pride was the predominant sin of Sodom that started the slide to perversion. Yet destruction of our nation, church, or person does not have to follow. God says, *if my people, which are called by my name, shall humble themselves, and pray, and seek my face, and turn from their wicked ways; then will I hear from heaven, and will forgive their sin, and will heal their land* (II Chronicles 7:14).

Prosperity Was Preached

Sodom's second sin was "fulness of bread." The people had more to eat than they needed, but rather than responsibly handling their surplus, they wasted it in riotous living. Statistically we know that the average North American consumes two thousand pounds of grain per year per person, five times that of the average person in the Third World. And it must be appalling to God to see the affluent North American consume in drunkeness alone equivalent to a quarter of the total diet of the average Third World citizen.

Privilege implies responsibility. If one believes the Bible he must believe that blessings come our way so we in turn can bless those who are in need. Paul says, *Blessed be God, even the Father of our Lord Jesus Christ, the Father of mercies, and the God of all comfort; who comforteth us in all our tribulation, that we may be able to comfort them which are in any trouble, by the comfort wherewith we ourselves are comforted of God* (II Corinthians 1:3, 4).

Prosperity is being preached in our Western world as never before. But, we must keep in mind its true purpose. Is this not what the psalmist prayed? *God be merciful unto us, and bless us; and cause his face to shine upon us; That thy way may be known upon earth, thy saving health among all nations* (Psalm 67:1, 2).

A recent analysis was made of the garbage of one great North American city. It was discovered that for every thousand pounds of garbage discarded over three hundred and fifty pounds was wasted food. This is especially tragic in the light of the fact that twelve thousand people die every day from starvation in our world.

No longer do we have the excuse of helplessness in the face of a hungry world. God has raised up ministers such as Mark Buntain of India who feeds eleven thousand persons each day.

Others such as World Vision, the Cambodian Relief Fund, and various missionary programs provide legitimate channels through which we can and must share our "fulness of bread."

Time to Spare

Sodom's third sin was "abundance of idleness." In North America we are able to earn our bread, provide homes for our families, and wallow in many luxuries — all by working about forty hours a week. Yet, in much of the world from the first ray of dawn to the last whimper of light, men and women slave to earn enough for a bowl of rice.

In India men compete with animals for jobs. They pull, push, and carry heavy loads to earn a single rupee. Many never live to the age of "retirement" and even if they did this is a word they would not even know. They struggle, scratch, and strain for every piece of bread.

Few of us realize the enormity of our blessing in North America. Our fertile soil, sophisticated irrigation, improved breeding, and nutrition makes our work load much easier. Thus we find large chunks of time on our hands just as Sodom did. They were in the "well watered plains." Because they had the time they sought diversions and entertainment. This led to perversion and destruction.

History is replete with evidence of boredom bringing perversion. Writing about the fabled Knosses people who reveled in riches and lived lives of elegant debauchery, Archaeologist C.W. Ceram says, "At the height of their development they had apparently reached a state of sybaritic decadence that contained the seeds of decline; for those who habitually lie in bed, even on a mattress of rose petals, in time will suffer from sores."

I recently visited St. Lucia with thirty-four of our church people. These men and women, some doctors and presidents of companies, had taken two weeks of their vacation time to help build churches for those who have less than we. While there Hurricane Allen slashed the little island and we found ourselves feeding the victims and ministering to their needs. This, I believe, is a creative use of our "abundance of idleness." At the same time about forty-four of our young people worked at a Mexican orphanage for two weeks helping harvest crops, painting, and fixing up the facility.

Perhaps it would be well to see our abundance of idleness as opportunities to give ourselves in such endeavours. God has raised up large missions programs such as MAPS (Missionary and Placement Service) to provide opportunity for personal involvement and proper use of our wasted hours. One man of our church is taking a two-year leave from his business to move to Africa and assume managerial responsibility of a missions printing plant there. May it never be said of us, *Woe unto them that are at ease in Zion* (Amos 6:1).

Sodom Spurned the Poor

Sodom's final sin was, "Neither did she strengthen the hand of the poor and needy." From the beginning we are emphatically told that we are our brothers' keepers. Sodom refused to recognize this responsibility and therefore had not great passion except to pursue pleasure. Without dedication to the great cause of bettering the life of all fellow humans, Sodom slid to corruption. The Bible predicted it because *where there is no vision the people perish* (Proverbs 29:18). Often a modern paraphrase is clearer: it says, "where the people have no great passion for a cause, they dissipate into meaninglessness."

Every church and every Christian should be deeply dedicated to the cause of missions. Apart from the command to preach and teach the glorious testimony of God's return blessing to them. There is a biblical reason for this: *He that hath pity upon the poor lendeth unto the Lord; and that which he hath given will he pay him again* (Proverbs 19:17). The simple fact is that one cannot "give" a missionary offering. One can only make a loan to God and God always pays back His loans with interest.

Five pronounced blessings are promised to those who care and give to the poor of our world. David records these by saying, *Blessed is he that considereth the poor.* Then the great king of Israel lists the five promises (Psalm 41:1-3) to those who care:

1) *The Lord will deliver him in time of trouble.* The Bible is a realistic book and recognizes there are shadows as well as sunshine. But for the caring Christian the promise is that problems are never terminal, only temporary.
2) *The Lord will preserve him, and keep him alive.* Specialists gave a Toronto doctor with a rare terminal disease three years to live. Now eight years later, he still survives and his physician friends are mystified. But this Christian doctor practices caring for and loving the poor, and God is preserving and lengthening his life.
3) *He shall be blessed upon the earth.* In *Animal Farm* George Orwell complained that Christianity offered only "pie in the sky." However, Orwell was wrong. Blessings are not delayed till death but come to us on this earth. Jesus said, *Give and it shall be given unto you; good measure, pressed down, and shaken together, and running over, shall men give unto your bosom. For with the same measure that ye mete withal it shall be measured to you again* (Luke 6:38).
4) *Thou wilt not deliver him unto the will of his enemies.* Although two world wars have staggered North America and England, still they have not been overcome. Is this because of brilliance or military superiority? Most feel not. The only answer that can be is that God has kept back the hoardes of the enemy since these three nations have led the world in exporting missionaries. As long as we care, God promises to preserve us. The same is as true on a personal basis as on a national scale.
5) *The Lord will strengthen him upon the bed of languishing: thou wilt make all his bed in his sickness.* God promises better health if we care for and love the poor. An immunity from illness is never promised but God did say He would give *grace and glory* (Psalm 84:11). Grace carries us through illness and glory comes in victory regardless of on which side of eternity we see the healing. All in all giving to missions and caring for the poor is not a bad insurance plan.

Such were the signs of Sodom. As a result perversion and incest resulted. It was one of the most sordid times in human history. Unfortunately some people learn little from the lessons of history and are bound to repeat them. However, that is certainly not true of all.

Isaiah talked of those who heeded God's Word by saying, *And the eyes of them that see shall not be dim, and the ears of them that hear shall hearken . . . And the work of righteousness shall be peace; and the effect of righteousness quietness and assurance forever. And my people shall dwell in a peaceable habitation, and in sure dwellings, and in quiet resting places* (Isaiah 32:3, 17, 18).

The call is clear. God's people must:

- Humble themselves and pray.
- Share their prosperity with the have nots.
- Use their idleness creatively in caring endeavors.
- Respond by being responsible to the needy.

The lesson of Sodom is certain. If God can only find a small remnant who will do this, the whole society can be saved. Our challenge is to be that remnant.

The Great Guest

Famed preacher-poet Edwin Markham truly captured the essence of Christ-like living when he told the story of Conrad the Cobbler. In his great work, *The Shoes of Happiness,*[1] Markham wrote that saintly Conrad had a vivid dream that Christ would visit his cobbler shop on a certain day. The dream was so real Conrad knew Jesus would indeed come so he decorated his simple shop with boughs of green. He prepared breads and cakes to serve the Master and then waited:

> His friends went home; and his face grew still
> As he watched for the shadow across the sill;
> He lived all the moments o'er and o'er,

---

1. William L. Stidger, *Giant Hours with Poet Preachers.* (Nashville: Abingdon, 1918) pp. 23-25.

When the Lord should enter the lowly door —
The knock, the call, the latch pulled up,
The lighted face, the offered cup.
He would wash the feet where the spikes had been;
He would kiss the hands where the nails went in;
And then at last he would sit with him
And break the bread as the day grew dim.

But the Master did not come. Instead a beggar knocked on the door and asked for a pair of shoes. Conrad hurriedly made the shoes and gave them to the poor man, rushing him off so he would not interrupt the visit of the Master. A little later came another knock on the door and Conrad was sure this was the Master. But it was a hungry old woman carrying a load of sticks. Conrad gave her the food he had prepared for the Master and helped her with the load. Still the Master did not come.

Late in the evening there was a final knock on the door. Conrad's heart leapt within him knowing at last this was the Master. But as he opened the door he found a lost and crying child. Conrad gathered the child in his arms and took him to his mother. Rushing back he hoped he had not missed the Master. Seeing things undisturbed Conrad knew the Great Guest had not yet come.

As the midnight hour approached Conrad knew that now the Master would not come. His sadness crushed him as he fell on his knees. From a broken heart the Cobbler cried:

"Why is it, Lord, that your feet delay?
Did you forget that this was the day?"

"Then soft in the silence a voice he heard:
'Lift up your heart, for I kept my word.
Three times I came to your friendly door;
Three times my shadow was on your floor.
I was the beggar with bruised feet;
I was the woman you gave to eat;
I was the child on the homeless street!' "